D1629919

1995

English Catholic Worship

ENGLISH CATHOLIC WORSHIP

Liturgical Renewal
in England since 1900

Edited by

J. D. CRICHTON
H. E. WINSTONE
J. R. AINSLIE

Geoffrey Chapman, London

A Geoffrey Chapman book published by
Cassell Ltd.
35 Red Lion Square, London WC1R 4SG and at Sydney,
Auckland, Toronto, Johannesburg,
an affiliate of Macmillan Publishing Co. Inc.,
New York.

First published 1979

ISBN 0 225 66262 0

Printed and bound in Great Britain at
The Camelot Press Ltd, Southampton

Contents

Contributors

JOHN R. AINSLIE, publisher's editor, former Hon. Secretary of the Society of St Gregory.

JAMES D. CRICHTON, parish priest (retired), sometime editor of *Liturgy* and *Life and Worship*, author.

KEVIN DONOVAN S.J., sometime lecturer in liturgy, Heythrop College, University of London.

NICHOLAS KENYON, script-writer for BBC Radio 3, music critic of the *Financial Times*.

MICHAEL RICHARDS, lecturer in Church history, Heythrop College, University of London, editor of the *Clergy Review*.

CHRISTOPHER J. WALSH lectures in liturgy at Ushaw College and the University of Durham.

HAROLD E. WINSTONE, parish priest and director of the St Thomas More Centre for Pastoral Liturgy, London, chairman of the Society of St Gregory.

Foreword

To be invited to write a foreword to this book about recent liturgical history in England gives me considerable pleasure for two main reasons. As a patron of the Society of St Gregory, I am glad to be linked with this jubilee volume which marks the fiftieth anniversary of the founding of the Society on 12 March 1929. I am happy, too, to be associated with a book which acknowledges the work of Dom Bernard McElligott, of Ampleforth, to whose inspiration and long-continued efforts the Society of St Gregory largely owes its existence

The choice of this particular means of commemorating fifty years of effort by the Society to promote greater understanding of, and fuller participation in, the liturgy, seems to me to be particularly apt. These essays fill a gap in modern liturgical writing by putting on public record information about the early days of the Society, about the people and events which influenced Catholic worship and development of the liturgical movement in England during the first seventy-five years of the twentieth century. Some sources are already irretrievably lost, but the authors of these essays have rendered a service by preserving for posterity information which might likewise have gone into oblivion.

These nine essays outline the changes and development of the public worship of the Catholic Church in England between 1900 and 1975—a crucial period. During these decades, the emphasis in Catholic worship throughout the world changed. Generally speaking, a ceremonial, strongly rubrical liturgy, celebrated by the priest on behalf of, and in the presence of, the people, has given way to a participatory liturgy expressing the Church as the pilgrim people of God.

England was probably less well-prepared than some other parts of the Church for this change of emphasis—as the book reveals. However, perhaps the most important principle, implicit throughout the book, is one that we have been somewhat slow to appreciate—namely, that true liturgy must reflect and express the minds and hearts of the people taking part. As is well-known, these seventy-five years of human history have been years of unparalleled change at every level of human life, especially in the social structure. Hence, the minds and hearts of people in 1975 were vastly different from those of 1900—their concerns and outlook spring from such an altered milieu. For liturgical celebration alone to have remained static and untouched would have divorced the life of worship from all other aspects of life. But liturgy, of its nature, should reflect reality and sanctify it. Hence it is necessary and right that the form we give our worship of God today should differ from the usages current in 1903, when Westminster Cathedral was opened. But, as with all change, human nature finds liturgical change painful, the more so because it is basic to life—thus no change can ever be final. The liturgy, like life itself, will go on adapting to fresh developments and new insights. But its core remains: re-presenting in each day and age the offering made once for all by Christ on the Cross.

Since this book commemorates the work of the Society of St Gregory, a major emphasis is on the importance of music in liturgical celebration. I very much endorse this. Indeed, I hope that this book and the continued work of the Society and of similar bodies will foster the development of music in English Catholic worship. Perhaps this book will encourage the skilled musicians of the Church to take up even more strongly the challenge of musical renewal of the liturgy. This, it seems to me, is a most pressing need, and I would strongly encourage English Catholic composers to apply themselves to this task. Something has already been done, it is true, notably by such men as Dom Gregory Murray, Colin Mawby, Anthony Milner and many others mentioned herein, but a fresh effort is needed to produce a variety of music suited to different kinds of liturgical celebration. There is a place for a choir, for congregational singing, for a cantor and responsorial singing, for antiphonal singing: all sorts of combinations... Such musical creativity requires no small degree of talents, sensitivity and imagination—but I cannot believe that these are suddenly lacking in the Church.

I congratulate the Society of St Gregory on its first fifty years of activity. May the next fifty see a flowering of the seeds sown by the founders, especially in the development of new and worthy liturgical music.

BASIL HUME
Archbishop of Westminster

Preface

The Society of St Gregory was founded on 12 March 1929 by Dom J. Bernard McElligott, a monk of Ampleforth Abbey. It has thus had fifty years of existence and this volume is intended to mark its fiftieth anniversary. During the years before the Second Vatican Council it was the primary means by which the principles and practices of the liturgical movement were made known in England and, within the limits of what was possible, put into effect. However its work is assessed, it had an influence on the Christian life and practice of the Catholic community in this country. In the essays that follow, an attempt has been made to see its work in the context of the history of that community; and only as much of the internal history of the Society has been given as is conceived to be of general interest.

To give perspective the book begins with the condition of the Church at the opening of the century. Three further essays cover the decades from 1920 to the period after the Council. Their authors are well aware that they have done little more than touch the surface of a subject which is vast and ramifying. It is in fact a pity that the history of the Catholic community in England from 1920 has not yet attracted the attention of a trained scholar. It would have made the work of the writers of this book a good deal easier. However, all facts and dates have been checked, wherever possible, and it is our hope that what is to be found here is accurate. One of the difficulties is that almost all those who saw the foundation of the Society have passed from this world and its seems unlikely that certain facts connected with the progress of the Society can be recovered. Even the origins of the Society are not well documented and the minute-books, then and later, tend to be laconic.

The sources of the history of the Society are of course those minute-books, to which must be added the pages of *Music and Liturgy* (1929-43), *Liturgy* (1944-69), *Life and Worship* (1970-74), and *Music and Liturgy* (1974 to date). From those pages it would have been possible to trace the different trends and some of the tensions in the Society over the years. There was the early and exclusive emphasis on music, especially plainsong; there was in the early 1940s the extension of the Society's work to a study of the liturgy as such; and even later there was the emphasis on pastoral liturgy. The very titles of the magazine (which has had a continuous history) indicate the different emphases of different periods. The tensions were predictable, though for the most part they were contained (if not always resolved) and the Society continued to do the work for which it was originally founded, namely to promote the active participation of the people in the celebration of the Christian mystery. The germinal statement of Pius X in 1903 has taken on many forms in the last seventy-five years and so has the work of the Society which looks very different now from the way it did in 1929. In recent years it has been reaching out for new forms of celebration, completely compatible with the requirements of the *Ordo Missae* of 1970 (as well as other documents, of course), and has in particular encouraged new kinds of music for our current liturgy. Interest in the musical forms of the liturgy, far from dying, has been greatly stimulated by the Constitution on the Liturgy and all that has followed from it.

This interest is partly reflected in the return of the old title of the magazine, as it is in those essays in this book which deal with the musical history of the Catholic community in the last seventy-nine years. Work of this kind does not seem to have been attempted before and, however incomplete, it may be thought to be of particular interest.

The last two essays, without pretending to be prophetic, consider certain possibilities for the future.

Since the contributors to this volume are all dealing with what is fundamentally one theme, namely liturgical practice in England in the last seventy-five years, they have had to use much the same material and there may seem to be some overlapping. A number of repetitions have been eliminated in the course of editing, but others have been allowed to stand since the various authors have used the same facts to illustrate their respective approaches to the subject-matter. One thing that has been apparent throughout is that it is in fact very difficult to separate discourse on liturgy as such from discussion on music. This may have something to say to us in our present situation as well as for the future. The new liturgy has often been pronounced dull, uninspiring and lacking in mystery. Few seem to have realised that the contemporary church has tried to graft this liturgy on to an old practice when 'low' or said Masses were the order of the day. In the history of the liturgy, a said rite has always been something of an anomaly, as anyone knows who has witnessed a private or low celebration of an

Eastern liturgy. The text of a rite is no more than a sort of libretto. It needs clothing, it needs 'producing', it needs all the help that colour, light and sound can give it. It is only then that it can be seen for what it is, and only then can it be judged.

Language, words, are of course equally important, but the English of the devotional services current before the council provided no model to work from. Translators, without a living experience of vernacular worship, of a liturgy that has to be sung and *spoken* and not merely read, have had to find their way towards a style that is suitable for public worship. It is not surprising that their first efforts have not been an unqualified success. It may be that in the course of time we (and that includes the consumer as well as the producer) shall find a style that it compatible with the liturgy. It may be, too, that the style will be of a kind that will stimulate composers to find suitable musical expressions for it. For in worship even the best of language calls for singing, for song that will lift up a whole congregation to proclaim the praise of God. Perhaps the Society of St Gregory, without ever lapsing into complacency, may regard its present emphasis on music as a sign that after fifty years it has lost none of its usefulness.

Of even greater importance is the formation of community, for it is local communities, of whatever sort, that celebrate the liturgy. Concern for this matter is reflected throughout this book and especially in the last essay. In this may also be seen an indication of the Society's continuing work which, by summer schools, publications and the search for appropriate musical forms, endeavours to be of service to the Catholic community in this country.

Those who have planned this book regret that it was not possible within its scope to do more than to refer to the liturgical reforms that have been taking place in other Christian communities in this country. They are by no means unaware of them, but those reforms are many and various and adequate treatment would have extended the book beyond what was practically possible. In any event, there seemed to be a case for considering the style, content and liturgical practice of the Catholic community in this century. To our knowledge it is something that has not been previously attempted and it may have its interest for that reason alone.

This book could not have been written without the help of many people. There are members of the Society of St Gregory, most of whose names appear in the following pages; there are others who have supplied reminiscences and information on certain details. Our thanks go to all these and also to the following: Rt Rev Aelred Sillem, Abbot of Quarr; Dom Laurence Bévenot OSB, monk of Ampleforth Abbey and composer; Fr Robert Murray SJ of Heythrop College, London University; Dom Alberic Stacpoole OSB, monk of Ampleforth Abbey (for valuable information on the life of Dom Bernard McElligott); Mgr F.G. Thomas, rector of Oscott College; Geoffrey Boulton Smith, lecturer in the music department at La Sainte Union College, Southampton; and the authorities of Plater College, Oxford—all of whom were kind enough to provide information on certain matters.

The book was planned by J.R. Ainslie, Secretary of the Society of St Gregory at the time of writing, Canon H.E. Winstone, Chairman of the Society, and Fr J.D. Crichton, who also read and collated all the typescripts.

Finally, we should like to thank Cardinal Hume for so kindly writing a Foreword to this book.

J. D. C.
H. E. W.
J. R. A.

1 Prelude: 1890s to 1920

Michael Richards

Every period of history is necessarily a period of transition and of preparation for the period that follows it, and can be evaluated in those terms. But such a valuation will almost certainly fail to do justice to the period under review, which will have its own characteristics and achievements, not all of which will have their sequel or be appreciated at their true worth in the years that follow. It would be a mistake to study the generation that preceded the birth of the Society of St Gregory and the liturgical renewal to which it contributed as if it were simply a stepping-stone to the higher things that came later, still less as if it were an epoch of darkness and decline before the dawn. I have attempted to avoid that mistake in these introductory pages: while looking out for the first signs of promise of what was to come later, I have sought to give an account, no doubt incomplete and inadequate, of the distinctive features of Catholic life as it expressed itself in public worship at the turn of the century.

The liturgy of the Church is never simply a reconstruction of the past, a piece of set pageantry whose *mise en scène* and costumes are for ever fixed: whatever means it uses, it must always be the straightforward expression of our own minds and hearts at the very moment at which we offer it. That moment leads us into other times, and into eternity itself, and it points towards our own future and towards that of those who follow us. The worship of the Catholic Church in England from 1890 to 1920 contained all these elements: it expressed the mood and the mind of the society that offered it; it introduced those who took part to the permanent and unchanging realities of their faith; and, both by accomplishment and by research, it made possible the developments in the midst of which we are still living.

From the beginning to the end of this period, the mood was Imperial. The public expression of the Church's life shared in that mood and indeed sought to establish itself within the Imperial setting. The period from Queen Victoria's Golden Jubilee to the aftermath of the Great War, from the heyday of imperialism to its nostalgic survival, strengthened by military victory, inevitably influenced the

1

frame of mind in which Catholics undertook their church building, ordered their ceremonial and even uttered their prayers. The young men of the time thought of themselves as vigorous realists, sharing with full-blooded enthusiasm in the struggles of life as members of the Anglo-Saxon race, 'the greatest governing race the world has ever seen... so proud, so tenacious, self-confident and determined, this race which neither climate nor change can degenerate, which will infallibly be the predominant force of future history and universal civilization'.[1]

As he planned the building of Westminster Cathedral, Cardinal Vaughan, whose own vigour matched that of his time, was very much aware of its setting in the Empire's capital and of the busy, expansionist mood of the public that he hoped it would impress: 'We desire that, at least in this immense capital of a world-wide empire of power and influence, in this great commercial mart of human industry, there should arise without delay a cathedral fully presenting the cosmopolitan faith and devotion of the Catholic Church'.[2]

The liturgy itself was not the problem; it was taken for granted that everyone knew what Catholic worship was. What preoccupied the Cardinal was the provision of a proper setting for it, so as to give it a proper place in the heart of the nation's public life. He was sure that his people shared with him the ardent desire that the Empire 'should possess in its very centre a living example of the beauty and of the majesty of the worship of God, rendered by solemn daily choral monastic service, as in the older...'.

In the context of his own time, he was echoing the hopes of Ambrose Phillips de Lisle, expressed in 1853 in a letter to Cardinal Wiseman:

> Nothing could more conduce towards the conversion of England than the establishment of a glorious solemn cathedral church in London, in which the Divine Office could be carried out with all conceivable glory and magnificence in a way worthy of England's past recollections, and in some degree commensurate with what so many holy servants of God bid us to hope for her future.[3]

The conversion of England and the restoration of ancient glories—these two themes were associated now with the Imperial theme, stressed by Winifred de l'Hôpital in 1919, when her *Westminster Cathedral and its Architect* was published. She described the laying of the foundation stone in 1895:

> Men and women bearing the eminent names of an ancient nobility, men distinguished in law, in politics, in literature, in

their country's service by land and sea, assembled to take their places in the seats reserved for the Founders and Benefactors of the Cathedral that was to be. There sat Henry, fifteenth Duke of Norfolk, Premier Peer and Earl Marshal of England; there the Earls of Ashburnham and Denbigh, respectively fifth and ninth of their lines. Among ladies, distinguished as much by charity as by noble rank, sat the Dowager-Duchess of Newcastle, widow of the sixth Duke, the Countesses of Cottenham and Mexborough, the Ladies Mary and Margaret Howard, Lady Mary Savile, and Lady Lovat, widow of the thirteenth Baron of a loyal and stormy house. Prominent in the ranks of our Catholic Peers and their wives came Lord Acton, the historian...

and so the resounding list continues, down to 'Mr (later Sir Francis) Burnand, the editor of *Punch*'. The clergy, in their serried ranks, entered to the triumphant notes of 'The War March of the Priests' from Mendelssohn's *Athalie*. 'The Canons of the Chapter of West-minster ended the procession, in which no women took part[1], the Sisters of Charity from Carlisle Place had already moved discreetly into the seats reserved for them behind the altar.[4]

The emphasis on hierarchy, both lay and clerical, and the pointed exclusion of women, went along with a sharp sense of social distinc-tion; the account tells us of others who had come, for whom there was standing-room only: 'eager pilgrims' taking their 'humble part' in the great occasion. Those who could sit down were Founders and Benefac-tors; we are not reminded of the contribution made by the traditional 'pennies of the poor', who had to stand.

The same reference to social hierarchy is found in the description given by *The Tablet* of the Golden Jubilee of St George's Cathedral, Southwark on 3 July 1898, but this time the classes are, it is empha-sized, able to mingle:

The Jubilee celebrations at St George's were made memorable by the ceremonial magnificence with which they were character-ised. Over two thousand persons, representing in their diversity all classes and every phase of Catholic life, were present at the High Mass. The free and open church had brought into close contact the Premier Duke, the denizen of the slum, the merchant prince, and the pedlar of the street.[5]

This awareness of the great contrast between rich and poor, whether the distinction is maintained on ceremonial occasions or seen to be overcome in the worship of the Church, is the next most striking feature of the society of the time to affect the Church's pastoral and liturgical style. General Booth's description of the human misery to be found in England's cities gives the background that any study of the development of the Church's worship must have, if worship itself is not to be sheer escapism and the study of it a frivolous amusement:

> What a satire it is upon our Christianity and our civilisation, that the existence of these colonies of heathens and savages in the heart of our capital should attract so little attention! It is no better than a ghastly mockery—theologians might use a stronger word—to call by the name of One who came to seek and to save that which was lost those Churches which in the midst of lost multitudes either sleep in apathy or display a fitful interest in a chasuble. Why all this apparatus of temples and meeting-houses to save men from perdition in a world which is to come, while never a helping hand is stretched out to save from the inferno of their present life?[6]

An appendix shows that the General could call on support from Catholics for his case and for the remedies that he proposed. At the Catholic Conference on 30 June of the same year, the Rev Dr William Barry spoke of the proletariat: 'those who have only one possession—their labour'... 'the homeless, landless, propertyless in our chief cities'. Christianity had not kept pace with the population:

> The social condition has created this domestic heathenism. Then the social condition must be changed. We stand in need of a public creed—of a social, and if you will understand the word, of a lay Christianity. This work cannot be done by the clergy, nor within the four walls of a church. The field of battle lies in the school, the home, the street, the tavern, the market, and wherever men to come together. To make the people Christian they must be restored to their homes, and their homes to them.[7]

Cardinal Manning had been thinking on these lines when he postponed the building of a Cathedral until the time when he had provided for the education of Catholic children. But his social concern—Dr Barry's words read like an echo of the Cardinal's address on 'The Dignity and Rights of Labour' in 1874—received due pastoral expression in the liturgy, as an Anglican observer pointed out after taking part in the Palm Sunday celebrations at the Pro-Cathedral, Kensington, in 1873:

> Though situated in the centre of the wealthiest suburb of London, the Pro-Cathedral has a large congregation of poor

among its regular attendants. They were, of course, represented
to their fullest extent on Sunday morning, and, as is ever the
case at Catholic churches, received equal attention, and went
away happy with as big a piece of palm as the wealthiest member
of the congregation.[8]

The fact that London's poor felt at home in Catholic churches was
also noted by an observer of the religious life of the time, C.F.G.
Masterman:

> ... In all central South London I have only seen the poor in bulk
> collected at two places of religious worship—Mr Meakin's great
> hall in Bermondsey, and St George's Roman Catholic cathedral
> in Southwark....
>
> In South London the poor (except the Roman Catholic poor)
> do not attend service on Sunday, though there are a few
> churches and missions which gather some, and forlorn groups
> can be collected by a liberal granting of relief.[9]

Cardinal Vaughan's concern that this should continue to be the case
in his newly-built Cathedral was shown in a letter he wrote to Lady
Herbert of Lea on 3 January 1903, explaining why he was allowing the
congregation from the Horseferry Road Chapel, which was being
closed down and sold, to use the Cathedral before its official opening:

> My knowledge of the poor, *unless the priests have them well in
> hand, unless the poor follow their priests, as sheep follow their
> Shepherd*, is that a great Church frequented by fine people and
> with the Cathedral character strong upon it, frightens the poor
> and they make it an excuse to stay away. It would require a priest
> with great strength of character, a priest who leads his flock and
> is not led by them, to overcome such difficulties, and draw them
> into the Cathedral after it has been solemnly opened and the
> great liturgical services are carried on in it.
>
> It would be far easier to attract them to the Cathedral, if they
> be first to occupy a certain part of it—if they be made to feel that
> it is theirs, and that they get there all and more than they are
> getting where they are.[10]

Rich and poor, priests and people, leaders and led: however much
the Church in practice bridged social divisions, they were obstinately
there, affecting matters of policy when it came to ordering the conduct
of public worship. It was thought of as ceremonial, so arranged as to
impress, to move and to console. Cardinal Vaughan's often quoted

words about the internal plan of Westminster Cathedral must be read with this social and pastoral attitude in mind. J.F. Bentley, the Cathedral architect, had put forward the thought that the primitive Christian style would be appropriate because it was not an insular one, but was a style common to all Christendom in the first nine hundred years. This fitted in with the 'cosmopolitan' emphasis which, we have seen, the Cardinal desired; but it also had a pastoral justification:

> A church of this type, with its exceptionally wide nave and view of the sanctuary therefrom, unimpeded by columns or screen, was without question that best suited to the congregational needs of a metropolitan cathedral, where, day by day, the Hours of the Church's Office were to be solemnly sung, and her great liturgies enacted, in the sight as well as the hearing of the people. [11]

The people were to see as well as to hear; their own share, except insofar as they were to derive spiritual benefits from what was done for them, was hardly thought of. Cardinal Vaughan wrote:

> We want to announce the glad tidings of redemption in Our Saviour's Precious Blood; to offer, without price, the exhaustless treasures of the daily Sacrifice; and to give to many a weary soul the peace and hope that silently distil under the unceasing melody of the Church's liturgy of prayer and praise. [12]

The liturgy was to be a performance: one with most important spiritual effects, but a performance none the less. Vaughan hoped that the quality of the performance could be assured by importing a community of Benedictine monks, Westminster thus becoming another Canterbury; in view of the idea that was later to be strongly held in Westminster that Benedictine monks were not appropriate persons to undertake pastoral care, it is ironic that Vaughan's scheme foundered on the fact that Prior Ford of Downside insisted that if his monks were to come to Westminster they were to deploy their energies in the parish as well as maintain the Divine Office. Vaughan wanted to confine the monks to the sanctuary and to their cells, and did not want to see them as rivals, however friendly, of the secular clergy in work outside.

The choice of the Byzantine style for the Cathedral was made out of pastoral and financial considerations and out of the desire to avoid the inevitable comparisons with Westminster Abbey should the Gothic style be used. For Vaughan and Bentley, it also had ecclesiastical and even political significance, as the universal 'early Christian' Style. In

1902, Edmund Bishop was to express his approval for other reasons: 'My own summing-up of the buidling is that it spells... the end of that romanticism which has carried so many of us to "Rome" and a good many to *Romanism*'. [13]

It was indeed a striking move away from the Gothic or the Baroque dress in which the Catholic body had expressed its faith during the nineteenth-century revival: a break with the immediate past in church building, like that of the end of the eighteenth century, [14] which was to be the start of a new and creative period. Indeed, the potentialities of Bentley's original use of traditional ideas from post-Reformation as well as early Christian sources have still not been fully exploited.

The ceremonial approach to the liturgy which for the time being prevailed saw it as a show to be put on for a people waiting to receive its benefits. The attitude was by no means confined to England. In 1906, a French theologian, Père Vigourel, defined the liturgy as 'the organized way of expressing official relations between God and man', rather as if it were to be classified along with court etiquette or with drill-parades on the barrack square. When Dom Lambert Beauduin began to urge the development of liturgical piety as the way to the renewal of the Church, he met with opposition from those who did not grasp the fact that his teaching was based on a profound theological understanding of the inner meaning of liturgical celebration. One critic wrote:

> In its most commonly usual sense, liturgy means, for everyone, the ceremonial, decorative, part of catholic worship, which touches our senses... since liturgy is only an expression in sound and image of dogma and faith, its influence on souls is more or less proportionate in the first place to the degree of belief and devotion and in the second place to the depth of emotional sensitivity of those who are present. [15]

Ceremonial could, however, be given a richer meaning and a deeper spiritual appeal, even if the enrichment to be drawn from a deeper study of the sacramental action and of the Church itself was not yet available. Robert Hugh Benson fervently proclaimed his understanding of the ceremonies of the Church as a very fine and splendid art, conveying its message in an extraordinarily dramatic and vivid way: '... The Catholic who aspires to count all men as his brethren employs every vehicle that his romantic brain can suggest: he batters the Kingdom of Heaven by five portals at once'. [16] He assigned the liturgy a place alongside music and painting, for the way in which it appealed to and united a great variety of people. His own literary work reflects the aesthetic movement of his time: Wagner, Debussy, Huysmans, the rich, exotic and mysterious. His poem *At High Mass* expresses this way of appreciating and drawing strength from the liturgy:

> Thou Who has made this world so wondrous fair;—
> The pomp of clouds; the glory of the sea;
> Music of water; song-birds' melody;
> The organ of Thy thunder in the air;
> Breath of the rose; and beauty everywhere—
> Lord, take this stately service done to Thee,
> The grave enactment of Thy Calvary,
> In jewelled pomp and splendour pictured there!
>
> Lord, take the sounds and sights; the silk and gold;
> The white and scarlet; take the reverent grace
> Of ordered step; window and glowing wall—
> Prophet and Prelate, holy men of old;
> And teach us children of the Holy Place
> Who love Thy Courts, to love Thee best of all.

In his life of Benson, C.C. Martindale showed that at that time he shared this way of thinking about the liturgy. A believing Catholic could quite well lack the liturgical sense, just as he might have no ear for music or be colour-blind. 'The liturgy may be, for him, no sort of desirable mode of expressing his quite real belief and worship.' The limitations of the aesthetic approach, built on a largely ceremonial or ritual understanding of liturgy, thus reveals its weakness, clearly seen by Martindale himself:

> A terrible tendency has declared itself to use that as an *attraction* which was once a *homage*. Frankly, altar candles are not there to give light; flowers are not meant to make the Church look pretty, nor incense to make it smell sweet, just as mitres are not for the keeping bishops' heads warm, nor copes for a protection against rain. The elements which make up ritual, having risen above the utilitarian, must never be allowed to collapse into mere aestheticism.

Somehow the springs of worship had run dry; Catholics in England had restored to the best of their ability and resources the whole setting and structure of the liturgy, but fresh inspiration was now needed. The very word *homage*, with its medieval overtones, used by Martindale as an alternative to *attraction*, reveals the impasse they had reached.

The Eucharistic Congress held at Westminster in September 1908 provides another indication of the character of English Catholic worship at this time. The outdoor procession of the Blessed Sacrament roused anti-Catholic feeling and became a matter for Cabinet discussion; Archbishop Bourne's diplomatic handling of the affair helped to earn him his Red Hat. The lectures given were either of an historical or an apologetic bent, in tune with the purpose of the Congress to manifest Catholic faith to English society, or else concerned themselves with encouraging eucharistic devotion and frequent communion, in the spirit of the decrees of Pius X three years before. But popular participation, even at Benediction, was at a low ebb. [17]

The work of Adrian Fortescue (1874-1923), parish priest of St Hugh's, Letchworth, and Professor of Church History at St Edmund's College, Ware, confirms this impression of the running-dry of the old sources of inspiration. In *The Mass: A Study of the Roman Liturgy* (1912) he set out its history as the best scholars of the day were then establishing it, but his interest does not go beyond the antiquarian and the apologetic. With his immense and varied talents, artistic, literary, intellectual and musical, he contributed with vigour and infectious enthusiasm to the Church life of his day. But J.G. Vance's comment in the memoir he wrote of him puts before us the same alternatives as Martindale was beginning to find inadequate, without yet seeing the way forward. Referring to Fortescue's love of the liturgical offices of the Church, he wrote: 'He loved their virtue of magnificence, their wistfulness and their splendour. His book on ceremonies, on the other hand, was written not to express any abiding interest but to secure a much-needed hundred pounds'. [18]

In his *Lex Orandi* (1903), George Tyrrell set down further confirmation of the way in which the future of the liturgy was beginning to seem problematic. 'The archaic language, music, and ritual has by lapse of time acquired a value, originally lacking to it, which now appeals to the historic and aesthetic sense of the cultured few; but what of the uncultured many?' And though he did not see how the advantages of enabling 'the crowd' to participate in public worship in their own right could be gained without sacrificing other advantages—'a return to primitive practice might be a return to primitive disorder'—he did nevertheless, by stressing the importance of the ministry of the Word as the first part of eucharistic worship, indicate, without developing the theme, one of the essential keys to later reform and renewal. [19]

The understanding of liturgy as ceremonial, with its aesthetic appeal or with its evocation in feudal terms of the Catholic order of the past, however appropriate it may have been to the mood and social conditions of the day, was not a sufficient expression of the mind of the Church to provide lasting satisfaction of human needs. Renewal would come from a deeper appreciation of the theological meaning of the liturgy, once the scholarly study of the documents had established a sufficiently firm basis for the work of interpretation, and from a realisation of the distinctive nature of the Church as People of God, independent of all other nations and kingdoms.

Already, in 1896, there were a few who realised what was required. Canon Barry, in whom General Booth found an ally, saw that the work of changing the social conditions that had created the proletariat and 'domestic heathenism', which could only be accomplished in 'the school, the home, the street, the tavern, and wherever men come together' required, besides the 'social' and 'lay' Christianity he hoped to see developed, a renewed theology of the sacraments and of their roots in human nature. Edmund Bishop, with whom he discussed this theme in December of that year, felt uneasy over opening his mouth to others about it, for fear of quickly being accused of heresy.[20] Such was the spiritual, social and intellectual atmosphere of the time; but, in spite of his hesitations, Bishop was to be the man who led the way in the historical scholarship that was needed as the first stage towards renewal. That he saw the wider significance of his studies, without feeling he was himself capable of working it out, or indeed that the time for such an achievement had yet come, was shown in the letter in which he told his friend Fernand de Mély of his talk with Canon Barry:

> For a Christian, a Catholic, living in the world as it is, the world of today, new light comes in from every quarter, bringing a new understanding of the ways of God, a new insight into the depths of Christianity, of Catholicism; and there appears already some idea of what the future will reveal in full evidence, how this divine religion is also *par excellence* the religion most perfectly conformable [*de pleine aptitude*] to the mind of man as God made him, and as he shows himself throughout human history.[21]

Comparative religion,[22] biblical studies, the attention paid to the themes of salvation history and of the 'mystery' of Christian worship; in these ways, the developments foreseen by Bishop were indeed to bear fruit in the twentieth century. But he himself was always reluctant to venture beyond that analysis of the documents of the past which led to a sure knowledge of historical fact; his own cast of mind, as well as the atmosphere of the time, inhibited any attempt at theological interpretation. The Joint Pastoral Letter of the Bishops of England and Wales, delivered on New Year's Day, 1901, is sufficient indication of that atmosphere; aimed explicitly at Liberal Catholicism, it reserved the domain of theology to the teaching Church, identified with the bishops; the laity were to acknowledge themselves to be the learning Church, the taught Church, receiving their instruction from the bishops and not venturing beyond their strictly lay concerns into theological matters. It took a further sixty years of the study of history and especially of ecclesiology to rectify this *simpliste* view of the division of responsibilities in the Church. Meanwhile its immediate effect on Bishop was to make him even more reserved and to provoke in him a temporary resolution to sell his books.

The association of the scholasticism of his day with the 'method of authority' made Bishop unwilling to grant it more than limited usefulness; the reaction against the liberalism of the nineteenth century had brought a hankering after points of certainty that tended 'to deaden the keenness of instinct for mere truth as such', as he wrote to von Hügel in 1904.[23] The application of the historical method to scholasticism itself was later to bring changes of the kind that Bishop would have welcomed; for while he had his hesitations over 'thinkers' and 'theologians', he had no doubts about the importance of the understanding that resulted from properly conducted research. In 1904 he was telling von Hügel that all his study of liturgy was aimed at the understanding of religion itself.

> The study of 'Liturgy' has been with me steadily gravitating to one side, which I may call the 'religionsgeschichtlich'. But for that, I would throw 'Liturgy' over altogether. It is not, other-wise, to my mind worth the trouble and the pains. And any seemingly bare and barren technical discussion of critical points is only, by endeavouring to fix the documents in their due time and place, to get into a position to deal, within a very limited sphere, with certain exhibitions of that '*histoire naturelle du sentiment religieux*', with the discussion of some '*type de reli-giosités*', which, with Saintyves, I believe will come, perhaps even in our times, to be the order of the day.

In the same year, in a Preface to a reprint by Burns and Oates of his article on the 'Conception Feast of the Blessed Virgin Mary', he wrote of the way in which his historical studies in liturgy shed a light on the process by which the Church reflected and eventually made up its mind about revealed truth: '... A general conclusion emerges, a formula resuming the whole history: first, popular devotion (an outpouring of often unenlightened but well-meaning piety) then rational reflection and discussion upon these productions; last of all, dogma. Those are the three stages. All his interests were concentrated on the investigation of this one topic, which shed light not only on *cultus*, but on religion—'and not only Catholic-Christian religion, but religion generally'.[24] One can see there a sketching-out of the way in which twentieth-century theology was eventually to be enriched, by moving away from the exclusive use of the 'method of authority' to a method that paid very much more than lip-service to the fact of the Incarnation.

It was his application of this method to the discernment of 'the varying natures, spirits and tendencies of the races and peoples that have found a home in the Christian Church' that Bishop saw as the key to the history of liturgy: without this search for 'the cardinal factors dominating the whole subject', that history would remain 'a hopeless tangle'. This was his outstanding contribution, earning him among fellow scholars the title of Prince of liturgists. Applied in theological studies on a still wider scale in later generations, it continues to guide our understanding of Christian reality in a way that the 'method of authority' could never do.

Bishop Hedley, the Ampleforth Benedictine who was Bishop of Newport, put the same point in another way, speaking as a pastor; his words contrast strongly with the mentality which, as we have been, so many of the church leaders simply took on from the mood of their time. They point the way unmistakably towards the developments of the twentieth century in church life as among scholars and theologians. In 1911, Hedley declared in the Preface to his book, *The Holy Eucharist*,

> We have, it may be said, now no Christian State. The pastors have lost their outward place and prerogative. The civil law makes it more and more difficult to keep up any Christian organization whatever... When Kings have ceased to follow Corpus Christi processions, when magistrates and knights no longer attend High Mass, when Bishops are no longer escorted to their Cathedrals by the chivalry of a diocese, the sheer frequentation of Mass and Communion by the Catholic millions must show forth Christ's earthly Kingdom,... Numbers, enthusiasm and intelligence must make up for pomp and patronage—even, if it comes to that, for glorious churches and gilded sanctuaries.[25]

The shift of attention from the public show to the watching people themselves, from the ranks of the rulers to the crowds of the ruled, from helping others *en haut en bas* to making available the means for them to help themselves, which will be increasingly characteristic of the thinking of the Church about its own nature and activities in the century that lies ahead, far from being a mere opportunist change of tactics, will be grounded in that serious scholarly study of the liturgy in which Edmund Bishop was so widely respected a pioneer. It is he who will, as far as England is concerned, show the way towards providing the new policy that Canon Barry and Bishop Hedley clearly saw to be needed.

Bishop's independence of mind showed itself in his rejection of most of what constituted the *raison d'être* and the inspiration of the liturgical activities in the churches of his own day. Ritual had been the rallying cry of the Catholicizing wing of the Church of England. By this time the battle over what Disraeli had called 'the Mass in masquerade', which had centred round the Public Worship Regulation Act of 1874, had been won, and it was realised that the Established Church could no longer be bound by the legal restrictions of the past.[26] Catholics had always regarded preoccupation with the niceties of ritual, particularly when it became the shibboleth of a particular party, with a certain disdain. But Bishop went a great deal further in his dislike of ritualism than this scorn of those who considered themselves as the genuine article for those whom they regarded as misguided imitators, 'Roman Catholics in all but their acknowledgement of the supremacy of Peter'.[27] The real crux of the matter, for him, was that the Anglican ritualists' defence of their case was far from scholarly; and his rejection of their point of view extended also to those Catholics who defended the use of ritual in terms of a romantic emphasis on symbolism and mysteriousness. The Roman Mass was for him distinguished by its sobriety, sense and simplicity, and he declared that 'mystery never flourished in the Roman atmosphere, and symbolism was no product of the Roman religious mind'.[28]

Between the mystical and symbolic approach to the liturgy encouraged in France by the work of J.K. Huysmans and welcomed by many in England, and the scholarly concern for historical fact of Edmund Bishop, there was a great gulf fixed. Bishop recommended Algar Thorold, who lent him Huysmans's *A Rebours*, to read also the later writings of the French convert's 'Catholic' period, *La Cathédrale* et *L'Oblat*, but warned him against the 'false mysticism of Solesmes'.[29]

Bishop's rejection of the theories and sentiments that lay behind the liturgical movement in France towards Roman standardization, associated with Dom Guéranger, was summed up in his comment on Guéranger's *Institutions Liturgiques:*

> For the ancient period, Guéranger is a mere *réchauffé* of ideas
> which later research and method have superseded; whilst for the
> latter period he is so passionate a partizan, and his work par-
> takes, in spite of its size, so much of the character of a party
> pamphlet to serve a practical end, that he is to be used only with
> an amount of caution and discrimination that implies almost as
> much knowledge of the subject as that possessed by the author
> himself.[30]

The way in which Bishop ultimately helped to bring about the vital
shift from the ceremonial, aesthetic or antiquarian approaches to the
liturgy, and from any use of it which fostered a two-class, 'clerical'
understanding of worship, and hence of all Church affairs, to the dis-
covery that it is the key to the understanding of cultural and religious
history and, even more important, of the perennial missionary and
pastoral principles of the Catholic Church, is clearly shown in his
famous paper on *The Genius of the Roman Rite*, which he delivered to
a meeting of the Historical Research Society at Archbishop's House in
May 1899. He showed there that in the Western liturgical texts of
modern times could be discerned the successive and distinct contributions of the 'Gothic', Gallican, Irish and Eastern churches as well as
the original Roman substratum. The ceremonial embellishment and
the baroque style that so many people associated with 'Romanism',
adopting them as party colours or just as passionately rejecting them as
unEnglish were, he maintained, not specifically Roman at all. The
original Roman contribution to the liturgy lacked the picturesque or
emotional character now associated with Rome; it was, rather, practical, simple, matter-of-fact and direct. One can see here not only an
awareness of what constituted the distinctively Roman contribution,
but a new readiness to recognize and appreciate the variety of cultural
and religious traditions which can live together within the all-embrac-
ing life of the Church. Once the serious scientific study of liturgical
history and its importance for the understanding of the varied achievements of the human had been established, the way was open for the
further theological investigation of the worshipping life of the People
of God from which has come the present, long sought-for, renewal.

Notes

1 Joseph Chamberlain, quoted in James Laver, *The Age of Optimism*, 1966, p. 230.

2 Winifred de l'Hôpital, *Westminster Cathedral and its Architect*, 1919 (2 vols), I, 260. Mrs de l'Hôpital comments: 'The imperial ideal, side by side with or perhaps underlying the Catholic ideal, as presented by Cardinal Vaughan to the Catholic people of England, together made a stirring appeal to faith and patriotism' in the very practical matter of fund-raising.

3 Quoted in Winifred de l'Hôpital, *op. cit.*, p. 8.

4 Winifred de l'Hôpital, *op. cit.*, pp. 2-4.

5 Quoted in B. Bogan, *The Great Link*: A History of St George's Cathedral, Southwark, 1786-1958, London, 1958 (2nd ed.), p. 304

6 General Booth, *In Darkest England and the Way Out*, 1890, p. 16.

7 Quoted in General Booth, *op. cit.*, pp. xxx-xxxi.

8 C. Maurice Davis, *Unorthodox London*, 1873, p. 383.

9 C.F.G. Masterman, in R. Mudie-Smith (ed.), *The Religious Life of London*, 1904, pp. 196 and 201.

10 *Letters of Herbert Cardinal Vaughan to Lady Herbert of Lea, 1867-1903*, 1942, p. 450.

11 Winifred de l'Hôpital, *op. cit.*, p. 25.

12 *Ibid.*, p. 260

13 N. Abercrombie, *The Life and Work of Edmund Bishop*, 1959, p. 282.

14 In *The Gothic Revival* (1928), Lord Clark described Bishop Milner's chapel at Winchester, opened in 1792, as the first to be built from Gothic revival motives.

15 J.J. Navatel SJ, 'L'Apostolat liturgique et la piété personnelle', *Etudes* cxxxvi, 1913, pp. 452 and 455.

16 R.H. Benson, *Papers of a Pariah*, 1907, p. 125.

17 *Report of the Nineteenth Eucharistic Congress, held at Westminster from 9 to 13 September 1908*, London, 1909.

18 J.G. Vance and J.W. Fortescue, *Adrian Fortescue: A Memoir*, 1924, p. 20. *The Ceremonies of the Roman Rite* went through many editions, the later ones in the care of Canon J.B. O'Connell, the widely-respected liturgical scholar who was later to guide English Catholic clergy into the epoch of Vatican II.

19 George Tyrrell SJ. *Lex Orandi*, 1903, pp. 43-5

20 N. Abercrombie, *op. cit.*, p. 258

21 *Ibid.*

22 *The Golden Bough* was being published in the years 1890 to 1915. But it was a long time before the significance for Sir James Frazer's work for the understanding of the liturgy began to be seen; liturgical scholars later did much of the pioneering work that was sorely needed in this field, with the result that anthropologists and theologians now find it normal to learn from one another.

23 N. Abercrombie, *op. cit.*, p. 319.

24 *Ibid.*, p. 337.

25 *Op. cit.*, p. xiii. Hedley echoes Cardinal Newman's insistence (in the *University Discourses*) that Catholicism must not be identified with any one historical period, or attempt to appeal to any one conception of true Englishness. 'We are not living in an age of wealth and loyalty, of pomp and stateliness, of time-honoured establishments, of pilgrimages and penance, of hermitages and convents in the wild, and of fervent populations supplying the want of education by love, and apprehending in form and symbol what they cannot read in books. Our rules and rubrics have been altered now to meet the times, and hence an obsolete discipline may be a present heresy' (*Discourses on the Scope and Nature of University Education*, Dublin, 1852, pp. 116-17).

26 The Royal Commission on Ecclesiastical Discipline, which met 118 times between 1904 and 1906, recommended the repeal of the Act, and the way was then open for liturgical revision within the Church of England and for the eventual granting to the Church by Parliament of freedom to order its own forms of worship.

27 The words of Cardinal Vaughan in 1874, when he was Bishop of Salford, quoted in J. Bentley, *Ritualism and Politics in Victorian England*, Oxford, 1978, p. 30.

28 N. Abercrombie, *op. cit.*, p. 10.

29 *Ibid.*, p. 258.

30 *Ibid.*, p. 273.

2 1920-1940: The Dawn of a Liturgical Movement

J.D. Crichton

If Great Britain had entered the twentieth century in an imperialist mood, it was with very different sentiments that she faced the future in 1919. Exhausted by a great war, drained of her manpower and heavily in debt, she was physically and emotionally ill-equipped to take up the great task of reconstruction that lay before her. British industry which had been geared to an all-out manufacture of armaments had now to be turned back to making goods that the world would buy. But in four years that world had changed a great deal and competition in the open market was keener. The economic difficulties that lay ahead could at least in part be attributed to the loss of markets during the war but the unwise destruction of the German economy in no way helped England. Nor was the political scene any more encouraging. If Lloyd George had won the war, his continued wheeling and dealing, his evident ambition and his failure to produce 'a land fit for heroes to live in' sickened many. Among other things he managed to cause a split in the Liberal Party from which it has never recovered. The Conservatives achieved power but the policies of that dreary Canadian-Scot, Bonar Law, did little to enhance the image of party politics. His most notable achievement was to bring Stanley Baldwin into the administration and thus introduce into the corridors of power a man who would have a decisive effect on the destinies of the country in the 1930s. As far as the Catholic community was concerned, there was little interest in party politics or politics at all unless and until the perennial 'education question' was touched upon. Hilaire Belloc's bitter criticism of the parliamentary system, amounting at times to denigration, was playing its part in breeding distrust in democratic procedures.

After the mini-boom of the early post-war years, the country ran into economic and industrial difficulties. Lost markets had not always been recaptured, wages were still low, the conditions of work often bad, and understandably there was a good deal of unrest. There were the police strikes of 1918 and 1919, there was the first miners' strike in 1921, when they were denied an absurdly small increase in their wages; there was the second in 1925 which was the prelude to the General Strike of 1926. This was a traumatic experience which the country has never forgotten; but if it failed in its immediate objective, it was a sign too little attended to by government and employers, that a new and powerful force had entered social life.

These events, and the intermittent unemployment that went with them, were of immediate concern to the Catholic community, for it was still largely made up of working people, many of whom lived on the edge of subsistence, and to whom the docking of a sixpence or even a penny from the weekly wage meant near-disaster. The General Strike was undoubtedly a national crisis and the Churches felt the need to make their voices heard. They produced an uncertain sound. The Archbishop of Canterbury issued a mollifying statement, though without much effect, but Cardinal Bourne of Westminster condemned the strike on the grounds of its incompatibility with Catholic social principles (the conditions of a 'just strike' were not fulfilled). His statement was a matter of contention at the time and has been since. But whether justifiable or not, it lost him a good deal of sympathy in the industrial North where he had never been over-popular.

Yet in spite of the General Strike and increasing economic difficulties, the 1920s were in some ways halcyon years. Memories of the war were growing dim; there was a somewhat meretricious prosperity, at least for a few years, and if wages were low, most commodities were still cheap. After the austerities of the war, people felt the need to enjoy themselves. Customs and habits had changed considerably during the war. Women had gained a new liberty—even the well-to-do could 'have a job' without losing caste. Moral standards had been falling even in the Edwardian era, and a popularized version of Freud (anathema to all good Catholics) had released many from their inhibitions, especially in sexual matters. Divorce tended to become respectable, except in Catholic circles where it was almost unknown, and homosexual practices—probably in part a result of the war—were prevalent, as so many biographies and autobiographies of recent years have revealed. 'The Bright Young Things' attracted a good deal of publicity (and the satirical pen of Evelyn Waugh), but their antics were confined to a comparatively small circle. All told, it was not a propitious atmosphere for the church.

The condition of the Church

If the mood of the Church in England in 1900 had been one of Catholic imperialism—later known as triumphalism—it had evaporated by 1918. The Catholic community could be described as the Quiet Church. If the over-optimistic expectations of the 'conversion of England' in the 1850s had given way to a more sober assessment of the situation, and if the flamboyance of a Vaughan had disappeared with his going, the community had lost nothing of its assurance and was very conscious of its own identity. It was still remembering the days of persecution, and it was held together as a tightly-packed group maintained by a clear and rigidly stated doctrine (the *Penny Catechism*), and an insistence on rules, customs and habits, inculcated by the clergy and an army of teaching sisters and their secular counterparts. You were a Catholic. You went to Mass every Sunday (or if you didn't, you knew you ought to), you abstained from meat on Fridays (though fasting in Lent was not felt as a serious obligation). You married a Catholic boy (or girl), and if, regrettably, your partner was not a Catholic, you knew that nevertheless you ought to get married in the Catholic church. The full rigour of the *Ne temere* decree of the Council of Trent on the iniquity of geting married before a 'Protestant' minister had been operated from 1908 onwards, often to the great confusion of the simpler faithful whose parents had got (validly) married in an Anglican church.

If you were able, you defended the Church and especially the pope, about whom you sang from time to time that he was 'the Great, the Good'. You spoke respectfully to and about the priest, though the bishop remained a remote figure. He appeared from time to time to confirm vast numbers of small children gathered in a large church. He kept himself to himself and otherwise made his existence known only when he appeared on a *Catholic* platform, usually to speak about the education question. For the ordinary people there were no difficulties; all was clear. It was all in the *Penny Catechism*, which all were assumed to know by heart from dingy cover to dingy cover. Limited as this vision of the faith was, it gave strength, though it also gave the Catholic Church—by definition universal—the appearance of a sect. In fact, it was an inward-looking community, and, if it had a whole range of organizations to look after the needy, it confined its attentions to its own. One reason for this is that the community was poor, there was no general fund, endowments were negligible, and bishops and priests lived off the offerings of the people. The Education Act of 1902 had brought some relief; teachers' salaries and the equipment of the schools (though not the buildings) were now provided by the local authority. Before that, Catholic teachers had existed on a pittance which they sometimes had difficulty in extracting from the parish priest.

Parishes were often situated in slum areas and the plant consisted of church (usually a diluted version of nineteenth-century neo-Gothic), school (a formidable heap of brick), and presbytery (often small and dark, with prickly horse-hair chairs in the parlour). Less often there would be a parish hall. All this had been built up out of the pennies of the poor, collected week by week, by bazaars topped up with 'raffles', to the scandal of the straighter sects. The community was usually closely knit, one generation succeeding another and the extended family a common constituent of the group. People knew each other, families cultivated each other, for this was one way of averting the horror of a 'mixed marriage'. In some parts of England you could be born, live, marry and die in the same parish without having any contact (except at work) with a Protestant at all.

But the war had brought changes. People had had to move here and there, there was the comradeship of the trenches, there was the employment of women in the factories, a general mixing-up of society. And the close community was being diluted in other ways. What we now call the 'inner city' was being thinned out. Even before 1914 the Church had been moving out into the suburbs; and, when council houses began to be built in the early 1920s, the movement of population began to gather momentum. New parishes had to be founded, the Mass had to be brought to the people; and it was a matter of painful experience that, if there was no priest to care for the people, some at least all too easily fell away. Mass was said in huts, over banks, in pubs, wherever a room big enough to hold fifty or a hundred people could be hired. Everything had to be created—church, school (usually the first to be built and used as a church) and presbytery—and debts were contracted with what seems to us now a magnificent assurance, though they remained a burden up to 1940 and beyond. Priests lived in lodgings and over shops and, when they had acquired a church, in the sacristy. Their income was often pitifully small. But the value of this unspectacular work can be seen by comparison with what happened around Paris and some other large continental cities. Dreadful shanty-towns were developing in the *banlieue* of Paris all during these years and it was not until the 'chantiers de M. Verdier' (the Cardinal of Paris) began to appear in the 1930s that some provision was made for these neglected and dechristianized regions.

Liturgical practice

The pastoral work of the Church, then, was going ahead, and the parish was still a strong element in the structure of the Church. But the circumstances in which so many priests and people had to live, the lack of proper buildings, the strain of raising money, as well as looking after ever-increasing numbers of people, were not propitious to anything but a minimal liturgical practice. It is difficult to detect any movement in the early 1920s. The worship of the average parish church had not varied since the nineteenth century. The staple diet of most Catholics was the Low Mass, said, without any music at all, often near-inaudible and sometimes (in the neo-Gothic churches) hardly visible. Only at the 'eleven o'clock' was there singing[1] and a sermon. At the Low Mass the epistle and gospel were (usually) read out in English (after the gospel) and the famous 'notices' were delivered, sometimes at great length.[2] The people were devout, and especially at the time of the consecration the church was filled with a sacred hush.

In addition there were the evening services, as varied in quality as in content, attended by an ever dwindling minority throughout the twenties and thirties. Here the 'devotions' were in the vernacular (more or less), and there was (usually) a sermon, and always the service of Benediction in Latin, sung to a very limited range of tunes mostly dating from the nineteenth century. Special Sundays, the occasions of the Corpus Christi procession or the 'May Procession' brought the people out in great numbers, though the latter was often better attended than the former. The Holy Week services had to be celebrated at times when working people could not attend, so these played no part in their lives, but Easter Sunday saw the churches filled to overflowing when vast numbers made their 'Easter duties'—sometimes, even in 1920, the only time in the year when they received Holy Communion. Yet there was a spirit of devotion—the English have always been devout—and those who practised recognized an obligation to live according to the demands of their faith. If these demands were conceived of as concerning only their own personal lives, that was the spirit of the time. Devotionalism meant individualism—the Mass was a devotion; it was 'my' devotion even for the priest—and this provided a great obstacle to active participation when much later it first began to be known in England.

There was but one sign at this time of a developing liturgical practice. This was the use of bilingual missals by the people. In 1915[3] Adrian Fortescue brought out his popular edition of the Roman Missal. This was almost wholly in English, only the 'propers', the Ordinary and the Canon being given in Latin as well. The introduction giving a little information about the Mass was brief and no other information was provided. Although it had a long life, it was soon recognized that it was inadequate. Some wanted everything in Latin and

English, and others further instruction about a liturgy that often seemed impenetrably obscure. This need was largely met by *The Roman Missal* edited by Abbot Fernand Cabrol, which provided long introductions, all historical, and as complete a Latin-English text as was possible in a hand missal. It appeared in 1920 and it too had a very long life. Somewhat later appeared the St-André Missal, prepared by the monks of that monastery in Belgium, which over the years grew to monstrous proportions. As well as the Mass texts, it gave Sunday Vespers, the rites of some of the sacraments, and other things as well. It was thus that the practice of 'following the Mass with the Missal' became common, though in effect it was but the continuation of an old English custom. From early in the nineteenth century, translations of the missal and even the breviary appeared (in spite of the prohibition of Pope Alexander VII in the seventeenth century!), and others continued to appear in subsequent years. But they were heavy volumes, inevitably expensive, and it was only the moderately well-to-do who could afford them. From the 1920s onwards, however, the use of missals, of varying quality, became ever more popular. It had two effects. Firstly, if people were able to take a closer, though still silent, part in the Mass, they became glued to their books; and, secondly, because the translations were somewhat literal and latinized, they got used to a sort of English that they thought must go with the liturgy. Hence, at least partly, the resistance to modern English in 1965.

Apart from this there was little movement. Fortescue's efforts seem in retrospect to be somewhat personal, though by his writings and his practice he did have some effect. He taught his people to sing plainsong—in his own manner, for he had theories about everything—and his Byzantine-like little church at Letchworth became known. His book the *Ceremonies of the Roman Rite Described* (1917), in the introduction to which he cocked many a snook at the Roman ceremonialists, helped many a parish priest and lay MC to find their way through the intricacies of the then Roman rite and to shape a seemly celebration. His own beautifully-drawn plans, the format of the book and its excellent binding (it appeared at what was probably the best period of Burns and Oates' book production) made of it one of the few books on ceremonial that has ever been published that was a pleasure to handle.

This phase of liturgical movement, if such it can be called, was in line with the current phase on the continent. The use of the missal and a very modest use of plainsong were the only means of active participation. There were, however, one or two signs that something was being done. At Ampleforth, where in 1915 Dom Bernard McElligott was put in charge of the music of the house, he gradually managed to 'involve' the boys in the singing of the Ordinary of the Mass and at other services. By 1923 this was the practice at Cotton College, too, where Vespers on great feasts and Compline regularly were also sung by the whole school. On the continent there was one further move made. In Belgium which, thanks to the work of Dom Lambert Beauduin, was in advance of most countries, a small beginning was made with the Dialogue Mass in which the people with the server answered his parts and said the *Gloria*, Creed, *Sanctus*, etc. with the celebrant. In 1922 the Congregation of Rites gave a cautious and not at all encouraging approval of the practice. It was more than ten years before it would make its way to England.

A weakness

In the 1920s, then, the parish structure seemed both secure and effective. For the parish clergy it was even something of a sacred cow. The good Catholic was the good parishioner, who supported his parish financially, who went to Mass in his parish church, and eschewed the dubious delights of places like the Oratory where a more exciting style of worship might be experienced. But there was one striking weakness. Throughout the 1920s and later, the columns of the *Universe* were filled with articles and discussions about the 'leakage problem': why did so many of the young, especially boys, fall away from religious practice when they left school? It seems a familiar question! Every possible cause was alleged for it, but on an impartial view of the matter it can hardly be denied that the style, and even content, of religious education was a major cause. Enforced memorization of the *Penny Catechism*, with inadequate explanation, or sometimes without any at all, and a certain regimentation about Mass attendance, made the young want to rebel. But there was also the fact that these children, usually from very innocent homes, were pitchforked into an industrial world that was crude and unchristian. One man, Fr F.H.Drinkwater, began a movement that was to have an effect on liturgical practice. When he returned from the war (he had been a chaplain) he determined to do something to improve religious education. His experience in attending the wounded and the dying showed him that men for the most part had forgotten all those hard and abstract answers of the catechism, but what they had remembered were the practical things like how to make the sign of the cross, how to go to confession, and what Holy Communion meant. He gradually built up what was called *The Sower Scheme* (later the Birmingham

Archdiocesan Scheme) in which the catechism was banished from the primary school, allocated to the secondary school and eventually provided with aid-books which would secure an intelligent learning of it. From the first he insisted on 'learning by doing', and this proliferated into all sorts of devices and methods. But he also realised that the Mass and the sacraments are things *done*, and thus he sought various ways whereby children at least could be involved in the doing. Much was to be made of sacramental events, and preparation for First Communion was regarded as particularly important. Teachers were urged to promote an atmosphere of happiness and encourage children to love their religion. All practices of regimentation, devised to get the children to Mass and examine them on Monday morning to see if they had or had not been, were to be abolished. There was little he could do about the celebration of Mass in the 1920s; but when Thomas Williams, a friend who understood his work well, became Archbishop in 1929 and at least *allowed* Dialogue Masses, it became possible to arrange for better forms of celebration. Needless to say, the whole scheme was at first far from the popular either with the clergy or with teachers, and there was much resistance. But Fr Drinkwater soon won over the training colleges (then all staffed by religious) and a new generation of teachers began to appear.[4]

Two other factors did something to stimulate the life of the community and would ultimately provide at least a basis for a liturgical movement. The first was a modest effort to promote theological discussion and the second was concerned with social justice.

Theology

One great lack in the Catholic community was the absence of a faculty of theology or institute of higher studies where theologians could exchange views and exercise the sort of scholarly criticism that is the condition of advance in theology as it is in other subjects. It would seem that those teaching in seminaries felt their isolation, and with the active co-operation of priests at Oxford and Cambridge, as well as religious (Benedictines, Dominicans and Jesuits), they came together shortly after the war and inaugurated the Conference of Higher Studies. Meant primarily for seminary professors, it opened its doors to others and met annually throughout the period, and indeed came to an end only in recent years. Papers were read, discussion ensued, and men teaching in different disciplines could keep in touch with one another. Some of the papers were published, especially after the foundation of the *Clergy Review* in 1931.

At much the same time the Cambridge Summer Schools, which again met annually, began their work. This enterprise from the beginning was open to all and its lectures were public. Among other things it provided an opportunity for seminary professors and other scholars to present their teaching in popular form, and to meet the challenge of discussion with the laity. Its great virtue, however, was that year by year it published the lectures of the School and provided some theological reading. The first meeting seems to have been held in 1921 when the subject was the Eucharist, and the well known theologian Père M. de la Taille, who had recently published his massive study of the Eucharist, *Mysterium Fidei*, was the principal lecturer. The second year was devoted to holy scripture, and there is little doubt that the fifteenth centennial of St Jerome's death (420) suggested the subject. It is interesting to recall that a long controversy took place in the *Tablet* about the feasibility of adopting the Authorized Version for use by Catholics—with, of course, the necessary changes. Mgr William Barry seems to have initiated the discussion at Cambridge. If the suggestion came to nothing (it does not seem to have been popular), it is at least a sign that there were a few willing to move forward.[5] The summer schools continued until 1940.

Social justice

Modern Catholics may be unaware that their Church in this country, *even* in this country, has had a long tradition of involvement in the struggle for social justice, as is of course also true of the Free Churches. The Catholic Social Guild—in which Mgr Henry Parkinson, Rector of Oscott College, played a notable part—was founded as long ago as 1909 in response to the social encyclicals of Leo XIII (especially *Rerum Novarum*) on the conditions of the worker. Over the years the Guild organised study-circles, which became widespread in parishes, and also summer schools, held at different centres though sometimes at Oxford. Then in 1921, thanks to the energy and vision of Fr Dominic Plater SJ, and with the enthusiastic assistance of Fr Martindale SJ, the Catholic Workers' College (now Plater College) was founded at Oxford. Students were drawn from factories and trades unions for a course in social studies for which they could gain a diploma. The numbers were always small, and there were those to complain that the men did not always go back to their factories.

Nonetheless Catholic social teaching was being propagated, and in this the Guild's magazine *The Christian Democrat* provided a platform for the voicing of criticism of the current social order. If it seemed over-cautious to some, its red cover and title spelt subversion to others.[6]

Both of these factors had an importance for the liturgy at the time. If, as we have learned in more recent years, liturgy is essentially pastoral, it yet needs a theological substructure; and though the Conference of Higher Studies and the Cambridge Summer Schools were rarely concerned with liturgy, they provided come theological stimulus which, when linked with the recovery in the 1930s of the doctrine of the Church as the mystical body of Christ, became the ground from which it was possible to proceed. The social movement helped people to move away from an excessively individualistic kind of Christianity and made them aware of 'community'. In fact several members of the Society of St Gregory—notably Fr Clifford Howell—were members of the Catholic Social Guild, and they came to an understanding of social Christianity and a sense of community through the Guild.

Signs of change

As everyone is agreed, the division of history into decades and centuries is a highly artificial one, and signs of change in the Catholic community began to be observable in the late twenties. The year 1929 marked the centenary of Catholic Emancipation; and, if the celebrations, High Masses, sermons, exhibitions and lectures were understandably somewhat backward-looking, the event led to a certain flurry of publications. Unhappily there was no serious examination of the Catholic past nor any attempt at an assessment of the intellectual output of the nineteenth century which, with all its limitations, had produced scholars and thinkers like Lord Acton and his group who had had the courage to raise questions about the Church that were both contentious and important. Apart from Newman, who is and was unique, men like Wilfrid Ward, Edmund Bishop and Baron von Hügel were all born and formed in the nineteenth century, though their influence lasted into the twentieth. The men who were continuing in the scholarly tradition, Abbot Cuthbert Butler (*Western Mysticism*, second edition, 1929; *The Vatican Council*, 1930), Abbot Chapman (*Studies in The Early Papacy*, 1928; *St Benedict and the Sixth Century*, 1929) also really belonged to a former age. Chesterton (who did not become a Catholic until 1922) and Belloc still remained prolific and were regarded as champions of the faith. Something of their rumbustiousness, rising at times to arrogance, rubbed off on a number of their fellow Catholics. But it was the younger writers— some influenced by Chesterton and Belloc and some not—who gave a characteristic flavour to the new decade. Douglas Woodruff, D.B. Wyndham Lewis and Christopher Hollis in differing degrees felt their influence. However, there were others who, while retaining their links with the Chesterton-Belloc group, struck out on their own. If a name is to be given to them, they may be called the Sheed and Ward group. With the energetic encouragement of Vincent McNabb OP and Hugh Pope OP, Frank Sheed (an Australian by birth and upbringing) and Maisie Ward, his wife, who had deep roots in the past (W.G. Ward and Wilfrid Ward, her father, the biographer of Newman) founded the Catholic Evidence Guild which trained speakers to expound Catholic doctrine in the market-place. If the emphasis, especially at first, was apologetic, the Guild had little to do with the Anglican controversy which obsessed so many Catholic apologists of the time. The Sheeds rapidly came to see that England was an increasingly non-christian country and that they must set their sights on the fundamental truths of Christian faith and living. Whatever may have been the impact on the crowds they spoke to week after week in Hyde Park and elsewhere, the Guild was undoubtedly an important means in educating a considerable number of lay-Catholics in theology.

Of no less importance was the foundation of the publishing firm known as Sheed and Ward. Catholic publishing had been respectable but hardly exciting, and the Sheeds attracted new writers and introduced to England a whole range of continental authors hitherto unknown in England. Among them was Karl Adam whose *Spirit of Catholicism* (1928—excellently translated by Dom Justin McCann) gave to many a new picture of the Church. Basing himself on a tradition that went behind the sixteenth century apologetic, and even beyond the Scholastic epoch, he showed the Church to be the Body of Christ; that, in a phrase which came into use much later and was consecrated by the Second Vatican Council, the Church is the 'sacrament' of Christ. In this perspective it was not difficult to see that the eucharist, the other sacraments and the whole worship of the Church were the expression of its deepest life. It was a book that had an enormous circulation and remained in print for many years and perhaps still is.

The other writer to make an impact was Jacques Maritain, the well-known Thomist who, it is necessary to say today, was a layman. Sheed and Ward published his *Three Reformers*, his *Art and Scholasticism*, known up to that time in a partial translation by Fr (Mgr) John O'Connor, his *Freedom on the Modern World* and many another work of his. If his *Humanisme intégral* (one of his best books) and his *Degrés du savoir* (his most difficult) were published by other houses, it was because Sheed and Ward had shown that he was an important thinker. But Maritain himself was only one manifestation of a whole new current of thought that was flowing in the church: neo-Thomism, somewhat disdained in these days, had a vitalizing effect on Catholic life. Thomism, which most had known in the pages of text-books (often described as *Ad Mentem Sancti Thomae*, and if St Thomas was any longer concerned with these matters he must have wryly wondered what some had been doing with his mind), seemed safe enough; but when it was shown that it provided a sharp instrument of criticism of modern life and thought, and when it was seen to be a philosophy that was concerned with human living, it appeared to be somewhat danger-ous. The French Dominicans liked dangerous living, and they put great numbers of modern questions under the Thomist microscope and found the usual answers defective. In their own way, and largely through *Blackfriars* (founded by Fr Bede Jarrett), the English Domini-cans did a similar thing for England. Links between them and the Sheed and Ward group already existed in Hugh Pope and Vincent McNabb—a notable preacher and public speaker—and the firm was happy to publish the first book of the young Gerald Vann with its sig-nificant title *On Being Human* (1933), for that was one of the problems of the day as it still is. In a word, to be Thomist at this time was to be progressive, and many did not like the direction of the progress. It was liberal, democratic and radical. The comfortable assur-ances of the conservative Catholic and the cautious reformism of the 'social' Catholics repudiated the new direction. Ordinary Catholics in parishes, if they knew anything about it at all, would have dismissed it as mere intellectualism.

Changes in parish life

Other changes of a rather different kind affected Catholic life more closely. Although the Great (economic) Depression of 1929-31 hit the Catholic community, probably more than any other, particularly hard, the advance of the Church into the suburbs and the outer suburbs con-tinued. The majority of Catholics may still have been workers in industry, but they were moving up the social scale even there. Skilled workers, foremen, works managers now formed part of the commu-nity, and yet others were able to found their own businesses and achieve a certain independence. Entrance into the professions also in-creased at this time, but representation there was probably proportion-ately still small. Such people with a modest competence, anxious to secure as complete a Catholic education as possible for their children, began to send them to boarding schools, convent schools and grammar schools, though these last had been opened to all who could pass the entrance examination (the 11-plus) since the Fisher Act of 1918. Although the community never had enough of these schools for boys, good work was done and the general level of education, including religious education, began to rise. This was partly thanks to an increasing number of the clergy who took degrees at English universities and often went back to the schools where they themselves had been educated. One result was that there were greater numbers of young people in parishes with sharp minds who were ready to question the *ipse dixit*s of their parish clergy. They often knew enough Latin to appreciate the Church's liturgy and readily used the bilingual missals that were now freely available.

Yet another change began to affect the pattern of parish life. In the 1920s the processes of mass production had produced large numbers of consumer goods that had hitherto been unavailable to the less well-off. The most important of these was the cheap motor car, the 'Austin Seven' and the products of Mr Morris at Cowley. The increasing use of the car meant that parishioners were more mobile, and at the weekend they took to the roads that were still for the most part open. Sunday tended to become a day out in the country, and evening services received another blow. The clergy might exhort, and even denounce, but the people went out. There was movement of another sort too. The new council houses and the private-enterprise building, of which there was a great amount between the two wars, scattered populations that had previously lived in quite confined areas. The housing estates were usually very badly planned; people were far from their familiar shops, friends and relatives, and they lost what sense of community they had once had. Apart from those urban areas where there was a great density of Catholic population, the old tightly-knit parish had become a thing of the past. The maintenance of anything like parish boundaries became very difficult and people began to go to Mass where it was most convenient.

New churches

Understandably there was a great amount of church building to accommodate new parishioners in this period, and most of the churches that were put up at this time mark a certain change in liturgical outlook. For the most part the neo-Gothic church became a thing of the past and the new churches were of a vaguely Romanesque style owing something to Italian models. There was usually one great nave which could enclose all the worshippers, for, if it was not yet agreed

that the language of the Mass should be intelligible, it was felt that the
rite should be at least visible. To see the altar and to follow the action
of the Mass was now considered highly desirable, perhaps necessary.
Sanctuaries, it is true, were often far away from most of the people;
and architects, or more likely their clerical clients, still insisted on
setting high altars against the curve of the apse. None the less these
churches that sprang up all over the country were an improvement on
what had gone before.

One or two tentative efforts to shape a church for the convenience of
the worshipping community should not go unrecorded. There was the
church of The First Martyrs built by Mr Langtrey-Langton in 1935
under the influence of Mgr J. O'Connor ('Fr Brown') with a central-
ized altar; there was the church of St Peter at Gorleston-on-Sea, in
which Eric Gill had a hand, where the altar was placed in the crossing
under the tower; and there was the as yet unfinished abbey church at
Ampleforth with its 'two-way' altar for use both by the monastic
community and the congregation of boys. They were harbingers of
what was to come.

In a related field there was another change. Perhaps thanks to the
propaganda of Eric Gill against debased industrial church 'art', there
was in the 1930s a growing feeling that *objets de culte* should no
longer be 'repository art' but should be worthy of their purpose.
Statues, crucifixes, vestments, the whole décor of worship showed
signs of improvement; and various objects made by Gill himself, by
Paul Lindsey Clark, and by others less known, began to appear in
churches. The chapel of Campion Hall, designed by Sir Edwyn
Lutyens, was an object-lesson, at least to the *cognoscenti*, of what
could be achieved with sensitive thinking.[7] The austere simplicity of
the Blackfriars Church in Oxford, with its wide-open sanctuary (really
a chancel) and its statue of St Dominic by Eric Gill, had a different sort
of appeal, greatly enhanced by the celebration of the liturgy according
to the Dominican rite.

Another feature of church décor is interesting since, in a very unecu-
menical era, it is perhaps the only example of an influence coming
from the Church of England. This was the installation of the riddel-
and-dossal kind of altar in many churches. It was flat, i.e. without
'gradines', and the candlesticks and tabernacle stood directly on the
altar table. Its front was covered with a frontal which matched the
other hangings. It clearly harked back to the English Middle Ages, it
had considerable appeal, and for the first time since Reformation some
Roman Catholic churches began to look like Anglican churches. The
frontispiece of Geoffrey Webb's *The Liturgical Altar* (1933, 1939),

which had a wide circulation, might well be the illustration of a (high) Anglican altar.

The laity

It does not always seem to be realised that the Second Vatican Council did not invent the lay apostolate. It already existed, and what the Council did was to show that the laity have not a contingent but an essential role in the life of the Church. The Church is the people, and its well-being and mission are as much dependent on the laity as they are on the clergy. The pre-conciliar Church discussed the matter in rather different terms. There was much talk and writing about the share of the people in the priesthood of Christ, and this was the basis of what was called Catholic Action, brought into existence by Pius XI. The weakness of the thinking was that the laity were regarded as subordinate to the clergy, even in those spheres of life where the clergy could not be expected to have any experience at all. But whatever the theories, it is surprising on looking back to see how much was being done by the laity before 1940.

First, with one exception, and then for only a short time, the entire weekly Catholic press was in the hands of the laity (as it still is of course). The *Tablet* did indeed belong to the Archbishop of Westminster, and until 1935 was edited by Ernest Oldmeadow who was thought (not always correctly) to be the mouthpiece of the Cardinal (Bourne). This was all the more unfortunate in that Oldmeadow, a convert from Nonconformity, stoked up the anti-Anglican controversy year after year.[8] Long before 1935 the situation had become something of a scandal and circulation was falling all the time. The new Archbishop of Westminster decided to liberate the church from such an embarrassment and sold the paper to a small group of laymen. Douglas Woodruff, a distinguished journalist and scholar, became editor, and gathered round him a group of writers who were almost wholly lay-people.

The one exception to lay-editorship was that of Dr Grimley, a powerful public speaker and a vigorous writer, though he did not always have that sense of responsibility when he had a pen in his hand that is to be expected from an editor and a priest. He was editor of the *Catholic Times*, which had a large circulation in the urban, industrialized areas of Nothern England, at the time of the abdication of Edward VIII. Grimley in great headlines pronounced that the abdication was a 'Bankers' Racket'. Such outspoken comments were too much for Church authority and Grimley had to go.

The *Universe*, after Sir Martin Melvin had bought it, adopted new methods and became a Catholic tabloid that was, and still is, very acceptable to a large number of Catholics.

In the middle 1930s a revitalized *Catholic Herald* acquired as its editor Count Michael de la Bedoyère, a very independent-thinking layman with a brilliant mind. The *Tablet* group were also independent, though always respectful of church authority—Bedoyère frequently was not. He was a liberal of the sort that, without malice, hardly adverts to the existence of authority. If a thing was right, if facts were facts, they had to be stated. It is not surprising that his paper was anathema to many of the bishops and clergy, and it was at times banned in certain dioceses and parishes.

The weekly press, then, was free and independent, and this made possible the ventilation of points of view that a clerically-controlled press would hardly have contemplated. Among other things, the editor of the *Universe* in the 1920s, and Bedoyère towards the end of our period, evinced an interest in the liturgy that in the latter paper led to a widespread discussion. Until after the Council the new *Tablet* showed little interest in liturgical matters; though then, and until his untimely death, Lancelot Sheppard contributed perceptive and well-informed articles on the subject. Woodruff himself was opposed to the liturgical changes, and after his retirement from the editorship freely made known his views in his weekly column.

The activity of the laity was not restricted to journalism or authorship, though the number of Catholic writers in the whole period was very high in proportion to the size of the community. It was the age of 'Catholic Action' through which the laity were urged to take a part in the work of the Church. Initiated by Pius XI with Italian conditions in mind, it always remained ill-defined and simply did not take on in England. Perhaps, by comparison with the continent, English laypeople had been much more active in their service of the Church, though their efforts were somewhat sporadic and uncoordinated. But Catholic Action seemed to many just a blueprint for more ecclesiastical bureaucracy; and, in the places where bishops tried to put it into effect, that was precisely the charge that supporters of old and (as they believed) tried methods of lay action brought against it.

But it is in this context that the movement known as *Jeunesse Ouvriére Chrétienne* (*anglice*, Young Christian Workers) should be seen. Founded in the early twenties, without any influence from the Roman movement, by Father (later Cardinal) Cardijn, it was intended to form young workers in social action so that they would be able to resist the pagan pressures of the industrial world and eventually make some contribution to Christianizing it. In Belgium and France it had, before the 1939 war, a very considerable success, and its members developed a sense of community that was translated into worship. The JOC, with its many branches reaching into almost every level of society, was probably the most important catalyst of what came shortly to be called pastoral liturgy. Whether because English young workers did not have the same sense of solidarity, whether by continental standards they had become somewhat *embourgeoisés*, or whether working conditions were not so bad, the movement unhappily never had the impact in England that it had in Belgium and France. Nevertheless the English members also developed a sense of community, Dialogue Masses were commonplace when they met together, and it is no accident that there was some collaboration rather later on between themselves and the Society of St Gregory.

For an adequate picture of the community in the middle 1930s other factors in the life of the Church should be taken into account. While on the one hand the young tended to abandon religious practice, there was on the other a steady stream of converts, often (thought by no means exclusively) middle-class. Many of them had read Chesterton and Belloc, Martindale and D'Arcy and Christopher Dawson. They came young (often from the universities) and in due course founded families in the outer suburbs. There they found Catholics of a similar background who had been to Catholic boarding schools or were sending their children to them. These people were articulate, independent, very different from the 'traditional' Catholic who lived in humbler circumstances and had not their advantages. Their relationship with the parish clergy was also accordingly different. In the old sense of the word, they were not 'good parishioners'. They sat more loosely on the parish institution, they had less need of it and were a good deal more mobile. Parish organizations were for the most part still kept going by working-class Catholics or their descendants. In worship the 'new' Catholics had different demands and often different experiences. Anglican converts sighed for the old hymns and the dignified language of the Prayer Book, those educated in boarding schools had usually had experience of the Dialogue Mass and the impressive music and ceremonial of the abbey church or the college chapel. The dull worship of the parish church did not appeal. In short, the Catholic community was becoming more middle-class and it was not clear that the parish was adapting itself to the new situation.

The clergy themselves had other and more urgent problems. They had their hands full with ever-growing parishes, and with new ones branching out from them. Usually they had financial burdens and all the time they had to organize various means of raising funds. Then in 1937 when, as a result of the re-armament programme, labour was once again in demand and the new Irish invasion began, the urban parishes often came near to being overwhelmed. Theology was not a primary concern, and the revitalized literary life of the community, the brilliance of a Waugh (whom many with Ernest Oldmeadow will have regarded as effete even if they had never read a word of him), the lively and sometimes provocative writing of a Christopher Hollis, the deeply-pondered learning of a Christopher Dawson, the way-out intellectualism of Blackfriars or of a Martin D'Arcy, were infinitely remote from the daily and pressing concerns of the clergy. But many of their people were interested in these matters and freely discussed them among themselves. For the first time since the Acton-Newman affair in the nineteenth century there was a danger of division in the community.

Other events were the occasion of a deeper division. All during the 1920s and 1930s the European dictatorships in Italy and Germany had been rising to power, and many middle-class Catholics were rather taken by Italian Fascism which destroyed the corrupt parliamentary system that had governed—or mis-governed—Italy since 1870. They were glad to see it go but did not see the dangers that lay ahead. Then came Mussolini's Abyssinian adventure, rapidly followed by the Spanish Civil War. The apparent involvement of Pius XI in the former caused grave concern among many, and Archbishop Hinsley's attempt to defend him produced nothing but the gaffe of the century. The Archbishop, believing that the Pope had been powerless to act against Mussolini (whom Hinsley hated), referred to him in a sermon as 'a helpless old man'. Pius XI was furious. He felt neither helpless nor old. Some Catholics held that the Pope was wrong and that it would be best to admit it. Others said that he ought to be defended and that was the general mood. But the really deep divisions in the community were revealed by the outbreak of the Spanish Civil War. Few, if any, approved of the Republican government that had indulged in church-burning, nun-raping and priest-murdering; but, when General Franco intervened and turned the situation into a civil war, most Catholics were on his side. On the other side was a minority, the People and Freedom group, *Blackfriars* (though not all Dominicans agreed with the magazine's policy) and *The Sower*, under the editorship of Fr S.J.Gosling. The wisdom, and indeed justice, of taking such a stance may be questioned—as it was—but when all the wrongs were attributed to the republicans and the atrocities of Franco's forces were denied, it seemed that the interests of truth rather than of what was thought to be the 'Catholic' view should be maintained. Whatever the judgement that is to be made on the matter now, it is a fact that the support of Catholics for Franco, expressed again and again in the Catholic press, did the community a great deal of harm. The charge that the Catholic church supported Fascism (and so by implication Nazism) was heard long after the Civil War ended.

There was thus observable for the first time in this century a division of opinion in the community that may be described as a conflict between the liberal and the conservative. The latter were in a great majority, though the former would increase over the years; and while it would be too much to say that the division foreshadowed the emergence of 'traditionalists' and 'progressives' during and after the Council (for some liberals were to be found among the liturgical traditionalists), it was a sign that henceforth no one uniform reaction could be predicted of the community. In ecumenism, for instance, modest efforts at dialogue were made throughout the 1930s and 1940s; during the war there was the 'Sword of the Spirit' movement which had ecumenical implications; but Church authority remained suspicious until the advent of Pope John. Even when ecumenism had become part of the official policy of the Church, many were excessively cautious and some hostile.

Liturgical attitudes

Much the same could be said of the liturgical scene. In all the period from 1918 to 1940, liturgical practice differed but little from what it had been in the nineteenth century, and even after the second and more encouraging decree of the Congregation of Rites on the Dialogue Mass (1935) some bishops forbade it, or allowed it somewhat grudgingly. Few if any encouraged it. A further sign of indifference to the liturgy was the appearance of a volume *The English Catholics, 1850-1950*, edited by G.A. Beck, then Bishop of Brentwood, in which the words 'liturgy', 'worship' or even 'devotion' do not occur in the index. Nor does the title *Mediator Dei* (which had been promulgated in 1947) appear there either, though it is referred to once in the text. In practice there had been some diminution of the English tradition of worship. In the earlier part of the period, it was the almost invariable custom to sing the principal Mass on Sundays, usually at eleven o'clock. As the Church moved out into the suburbs, as makeshift buildings had to be used for churches, and as the clergy became more and more burdened with debts and increasing numbers of people, the regular sung Mass became less and less common. Nor did the promotion of plainchant do much to help the situation. It seems to be forgotten that there was a considerable animus against plainchant; and, when zealous priests enforced its singing and replaced the old figured music with it, they had trouble with their choirs and many were disbanded. *Plus ça change....*!

Another factor that affected liturgical attitudes, and one to which too little attention has been paid, was the promulgation of the Code of Canon Law in 1918—a handy volume, as its title indicates, of Church law that affected every department of Church life. As lawyers trained in its interpretation took up their places in the dioceses, and as the requirements of the Code were brought to bear, especially on the clergy, a new legalist mentality invaded the community. Since the new Code was by no means as perspicuous as its compilers had intended it to be, recourse to Rome for the solution of problems became ever more common. A similar trend invaded the sphere of rubrics, the correct performance of which was identified with 'liturgy'; but since even in the elaborate rubrical code of the Pius V Missal there continued to be obscurities (or what the pernickety chose to regard as such), the Congregation of Rites was kept very busy answering the questions of bishops and ceremonialists throughout the Church. The rubricians had indeed a continual field-day. All this and much more made the community look very Rome-centred in a way that it had not been even at the height of Manning's ultramontanism.

One unfortunate result of this barrage of legislation, and the spirit behind it, was that venerable customs tended to disappear. 'Gothic' or Pugin-designed vestments had been used in some places for a very long time and then some purist came along and threw them out as not being 'Roman'. The *Ordo Administrandi Sacramenta*, compiled by the learned and saintly Bishop Challoner in the eighteenth century, tended to disappear (except for marriage, for which we had retained the Sarum rite) and to be replaced by the *Rituale Romanum* which was never intended to have the same status as the breviary and the missal of Pius V. Few seemed to realise that the homilies in the *Ordo* for baptisms, marriages, the administration of the sacraments of the sick and the care of the dying had been written by Challoner, all in accordance with the requirements of the Council of Trent! In this the *Ordo* was far more up to date than the *Rituale Romanum*. Again, no care was taken to preserve certain English customs that went back to Penal days. For at least two centuries the dead had been buried in English, but the canonists and the rubricians frowned on this, and mourners went away unconsoled by the slabs of Latin that assaulted their ears, for in the early part of this period they did not have even the consolation of the Requiem Mass. Like the Nuptial Mass, it was regarded as the privilege of the well-to-do. In spite of the insistence on rubrics and the increasing romanization of the liturgy, ironically enough the clergy largely went their own way. Obsession with rubrical prefection did secure a certain dignity in worship (even if it did not communicate much) but complaints about bad celebration were prevalent throughout the period (the missal-users 'could not keep up with the priest') and far beyond it.

The age of perfervid Italianate devotions had largely passed away and the residue did not seem more attractive now that the fervour had gone. *The Manual of Prayers*, derived from a re-edition of an even earlier book by Challoner, had by 1920 agglutinated to itself the texts of a number of 'devotions', the language of which, in the words of Evelyn Waugh, 'was in places stilted to the point of indecorum'.[9] Cardinal Hinsley set up a committee to revise it, and Ronald Knox was commissioned to translate those texts whose originals were Latin or Italian. The work gave him nothing but trouble and no satisfaction. When it appeared, there were public complaints about inaccurate information on indulgences (which were no concern of his), and about certain directives; and there was a Latin howler which had escaped the notice of the episcopal editors. The book was withdrawn (i.e. the bishops had to buy it back from the publishers), ostensibly because of these errors but *in fact* because most of the clergy did not like it. They had entertained the illusion that the language of the former book was old, venerable, even Elizabethan; and, when Knox produced some excellent pastiches of Elizabethan prayers, they rejected them. Perhaps they smelt of the Book of Common Prayer. The incident is of little importance now but it reveals how very conservative the clergy were. The same fate overtook yet another edition which Mgr H.F. Davis, then Vice-Rector of Oscott College, was asked to edit. He retained almost all the old texts but gathered new material from various sources, especially the excellent German diocesan prayer-books. It would have made a valuable contribution to English worship if it had ever appeared. The bishops just threw it out. The last attempt at a vernacular set of devotions was conservative in every sense and was edited by a bishop.

The beginnings of a liturgical movement

The Catholic community suffered diminution in another sense. The great liturgiologist, Edmund Bishop, a layman, had died in 1917; and his *Liturgica Historica*, edited by his friend, Dom Hugh Connolly of

Downside, which appeared in 1918, was a monument to his life's work which in some respects had been epoch-making. He had no successors. Connolly, a specialist in Syriac literature, brought out his edition, still the best, of the *Didascalia Apostolorum* in 1929; and right at the end of the period published papers to show that the *De Sacramentis*, sometimes attributed to St Ambrose, was indeed his work. His view has since been endorsed by continental scholars (Botte, Faller....). Herbert Thurston SJ had in the past made useful contributions to liturgical history but no major work came from him in this period, although he did something to keep Fortescue's book *The Mass* alive by adding a new bibliography in 1937. Fortescue himself died, at a tragically early age, in 1923; and, though most of his work had been done before 1918, his missal remained in circulation, as did sundry pamphlets of his published by the Catholic Truth Society.

The scholarship of the French monks of Farnborough cannot be claimed by English Catholics, though they were the beneficiaries of it. The Cabrol Missal (as it came to be called) was widely used, and some of the work of the Farnborough monks appeared in translation, notably Cabrol's *The Mass of the Western Rites*. The large *Dictionnaire d'Archéologie Chrétienne et de Liturgie* (the order of words in the title is significant), edited by Fernand Cabrol and Henri Leclercq (who, greatly to its detriment, wrote the second half almost single-handed), was proceeding at the time but was consulted only by specialists.

Liturgical publication increased in the 1930s and it will be convenient to make some mention of it here. The first volume of *The Church's Year*, mostly historical, came in 1938 from the pen of the by now veteran liturgist, Fernand Cabrol; and Dom Ernest Graf's little book, *The Church's Daily Prayer*, which appeared about the same time was, with Battifol's *History of the Breviary* (E.T. 1912), the only material available on the Divine Office.[10] Other books showed a different approach and began to provide some theological basis for liturgical study and practice. The first was Romano Guardini's *Spirit of the Liturgy*, translated from the German and published by Sheed and Ward (1930). It brought some freshness to English thinking on the subject, and was welcomed by those already interested in the liturgy, though his emphasis on *logos* rather than *ethos* left some baffled and others cold. Dom Theodore Wesseling's *Liturgy and Life* (1937) introduced Dom Odo Casel's thought to English readers (though I do not think that his name appears in the book), and there were some, including bishops, who looked askance at what they regarded as his panliturgism. What he was concerned about was the nature of the

Christian Mystery and its celebration by the community. Right at the end of the period came the work of Maurice Zundel, *The Splendour of the Liturgy*, which was rather a theological meditation on the liturgy than a study of it. Lastly, a native writer, Fr Antony Thorold, published his *Mass and the Life of Prayer* in which he showed that the Mass when rightly understood demanded active participation and was in no way inimical to private prayer.

In periodical literature there was *Music and Liturgy*, the organ of the newly-founded Society of St Gregory, the *Magnificat* which published articles on the Divine Office and the Liturgical Year, and *Orate Fratres* (now *Worship*), edited in lively fashion by Dom Virgil Michel from St John's Abbey, Collegeville, Minnesota, which had its readers in England. This volume of publication, though not spectacular, would seem to indicate that there was a good deal of interest in the liturgy at least in the last years of our period.

Rather earlier, a very different sort of writer began to give a practical impetus to the liturgical movement. Cyril Martindale would have been the last to make any claim to liturgical scholarship but for many years he evinced a strong interest in the matter of worship. He was always close to people; he knew what they were thinking and what they wanted. A first-rate classical scholar, he acquired a growing interest in the texts of the Latin liturgy which, however, he realised was a barrier to an understanding of and participation in the Mass for the dockers, miners and boxers among whom he chose to work. With typical energy and practicality over the years he produced a series of books and booklets that were devised to make the liturgy intelligible and usable to those who would read them. In 1929 appeared his little book *The Mind of the Missal*, one of the few books on the subject written in such fashion as to appeal to the non-specialist. Based (alas) on insufficient scholarship, it gave a summary history of the Mass and, what was perhaps more valuable, he translated (in his own inimitable style) and commented on the texts of the great seasons and feasts. Here, and in his *Words of the Missal*, as well as further booklets on the prayers of the Mass, he endeavoured to make their meaning plain. It was an obvious, simple yet fundamental thing to do, for too many were content to regard the contents of the liturgical books as so much sacred mumbo-jumbo. In addition, he published a number of pamphlets giving translations of Compline and the offices of Holy Week (*Tenebrae*). It should not go unrecorded here that he was an early friend and constant supporter of the work of the Society of St Gregory.

Liturgical movement

The publication of books is one thing, practice is another; and, within the limits of what was possible, something was done. As will be more fully recounted elsewhere[11] the *Motu proprio* of Pius X in 1903 and the restoration of the Gregorian chant and the books that contained it, notably the *Graduale* (the *Antiphonale Romanum* hung fire and was in fact never completed), gave an impetus to the singing of the chant in almost every part of the church. If a little group of pilgrims from Calabria sang a barely recognizable version of the *Salve Regina* in Rome in 1950, it meant that someone long ago had tried to implement the instructions of Pius X. The *Missa de Angelis* (the *Kyrie, Gloria* and *Agnus* of which are of very dubious parentage) became widely known, though in the 1920s it was usually sung by the choir. In an endeavour to be obedient to the Holy See, a good deal of pressure had been brought to bear on the singing of the chant. In fact, there was a danger, not always avoided, that the singing of the chant would become an end in itself. There were festivals of plainsong here and there; there were also *children's* festivals of plainsong, though one had to ask oneself when and where they exercised their expertise liturgically. But a more respectable reason for these campaigns was the view that a 'liturgical' Mass was one sung in plainsong and the *Motu proprio* could be quoted in its support. The emphasis on music in that document was certainly very strong, and at first few if any noticed the statement in it that active participation in the liturgy is the chief source of the Christian spirit—a surprising, and as it proved a prophetic, statement that came in an age when most people would have said that private prayer, devotions and other practices of piety were the chief source of that spirit. Among the few who did notice the statement and realised some of its possibilities was Dom Lambert Beauduin, a monk of Mont-César, who, not without difficulty, launched the *pastoral* liturgical movement in Belgium in 1909. By instruction, by propaganda in *La Vie liturgique* (which he founded in 1909, later (1911) *Questions liturgiques* and in 1919 *Questions liturgiques et paroissiales*) and by conferences he spread notions about a liturgy in which people could and should take part. In his *Piété de l'Église* he provided a theological foundation for the practice he was urging, the basis of it being the people's share in the priesthood of Christ. A good deal of the book was taken up into the encyclical *Mediator Dei*, though no doubt on account of the war it was never published in translation in England.[12] It long remained unknown in England, which was thus deprived of a theological *rationale* for a liturgical movement that was just beginning.

Even in Belgium and France, however, the liturgical movement was making slow progress, for the effect of Beauduin's work was cumulative rather than instantaneous. Plainsong, which was actively promoted in France, the home of the Solesmes experts, was still seen as the only means whereby people could be drawn into the action of the liturgy. In Germany, at Maria Laach, Abbot Herwegen and Dom Odo Casel were creating a centre of liturgical study, and in the same country Romano Guardini was speaking about liturgy to large gatherings of young people. But it was in Austria at Klosterneuburg that a liturgy-for-the-people, *Volksliturgie*, under the energetic and well-informed Pius Parsch, got off the ground. Relying on the even-then long tradition in German-speaking lands of the use of the vernacular even in the official liturgy, he provided a whole series of texts that could be used in its celebration. His work, too, was unknown in England until after the Second World War.

Some tradition of singing plainchant, and some, few, attempts to engage the congregation in singing it—such was the liturgical situation in England when Pius XI published his constitution, *Divini Cultus*, in 1928. This document, too, was principally about church music, but it took up his predecessor's injunction about active participation in no uncertain terms and urged it anew. The people were not to be silent and remote spectators of the sacred rites: they were to take an active part, responding to the celebrant and singing with the choir as the case might be. Like his predecessor, he made strong recommendations that the singing of the Gregorian chant should be taught everywhere and *used*. Pius XI was a practical man. His vision was that of a whole congregation singing the Mass, and if he nowhere refers to the Dialogue Mass (which was already in use on the Continent) the principles he laid down were valid for that also, as some at least began to see.

The foundation of the Society of St Gregory

Among the few who had taken note of the importance and potentiality of Pius X's phrase about active participation was a monk of Ampleforth, Dom Bernard McElligott. As will be seen from what has been said above, he had already been concerned with the music of the monastery and school, and his first desire was to do something more generally for church music. In a letter to the *Universe* (2 November 1928) he voiced his concerns, and that letter attracted some eighty replies. In March 1929 he called a meeting at St Benedict's Priory, Ealing, and thirty people attended. It was there and then decided to found a society to 'maintain the dignity of the sacred liturgy as the supreme instrument of congregational worship' and 'to carry out the wishes of the church with regard to church music' as given in the papal documents. Thus came into existence the Society of St Gregory on 12 March 1929, the feast-day of the saint. The meeting decided at once to hold a summer school in Oxford the same year, when '85 members met at Blackfriars, Oxford (in August), Pius XI and the sister Society in America sending cables of goodwill'.[13]

Between the original letter to the *Universe* and the calling of the meeting in 1929, the Apostolic Constitution on music of Pius XI had appeared. This considerably strengthened McElligott's case. Although the words 'active participation' do not appear in the 'Four Aims' of the Society as they were at first formulated,[14] the theme is implicit in the phrase 'instrument of *congregational* singing'. In any case Dom Bernard was never tired of repeating the statement that active participation in the liturgy is the supreme and indispensable source of the Christian spirit. In the middle 1930s, when he was chaplain to the Eric Gills at Pigotts, he contributed to the *Catholic Herald* a series of articles on liturgical music which had a strongly congregational slant. His mind is revealed in the title of the series, 'The Liturgy and the People', and in that of one of the articles, 'Three Voices: Clergy, Choir and People'. To rebut the charge that his work and that of the Society was esoteric, 'he never ceased to preach the congregational amateur value as *eo ipso* superior as praise if not as music to that of the professional choir'.[15]

If we are to judge by patronage and numbers, the Society met with an immediate success. Patrons included Cardinal Bourne, two other archbishops, eight bishops and by 1930, the Abbots of Solesmes and Farnborough. Membership at the time of the first summer school stood at 223 and a further 120 members were added by July, 1930. Religious communities of women (the enclosed orders being 'praying members', among whom Stanbrook was probably the first) and choirs were affiliated to the Society. The series of summer schools, held annually until 1940, and the inauguration of the Society's quarterly in 1929, made the work of the Society more widely known. Although pronounced by some to be élitist, and never liked by the tough guys whether ecclesiastical or lay, it could be said to have given expression to a certain desire for an improvement in the standards of public worship in general and of music in particular.

Although at the first summer school there had been two non-musical lectures, by the editor of the *Tablet* (Oldmeadow) and the *Universe* (Dean) respectively, until 1942 the Society was almost wholly concerned with the singing of the Gregorian chant. The reasons for this were, first, that, although it was of course not unknown, the manner of singing it left much to be desired; and secondly, because it was seen to be the means, at that time the only means, of securing the active participation of the people. Such indeed from the beginning was the intention. It was all in the papal documents. Moreover, it was 'safe', for no one in the face of the clear statements in those documents could object to people *singing*. It is not clear why authority (later) objected to them *saying*. But at first the Society did not concern itself with these or other purely liturgical issues. As one of the first members, Dom Laurence Bévenot, has said: '[Until 1942] it had been assumed that the significance of the liturgy did not need explaining!' There is something to be said for that point of view: the liturgy is primarily something to be *done*, not something to be talked about. But, alas, the liturgy as it then was could be described for many as a *maquis impénétrable*, an impenetrable thicket, that did in fact need a good deal of explanation. For want of an understanding of the basic shape of the Mass, for instance, even methods of participation could and did go astray. When later the Dialogue Mass came into use there were those who did not know what the people should properly be asked to say and what not. They were asked, urged, to respond with the server to the introductory psalm, the *Iudica*, an almost impossible task for the non-Latinist; and there were others who recommended that the (private) prayers of the offertory should be said by the congregation, in English of course.

Throughout the 1930s the Society went on its way, holding its annual summer schools at Oxford, and gradually gathering support, though almost always from musicians. It also became the object of criticism, even from some of its own members. It was criticised for its commitment to the Solesmes method of singing the chant. There were those who complained that the Society neglected polyphony and modern music. There were also internal administrative difficulties. A Society was in formation, and it is not surprising that McElligott and his supporters were not able to strike the right balance all at once. There was criticism from outside the Society which found itself running against a quite strong current of opinion summed up in the slogan, so often heard in ecclesiastical affairs, *quieta non movere*, 'not to be disturbed'. However, the work of the Society spread. The training colleges were welcoming, and there was even some penetration of parish life. Bernard McElligott was invited to parishes where he gave 'liturgical missions' during which he taught the principles of active participation, and in the space of a week did something to secure it. Other members of the Society were active in choirs and schools.

In 1935 another event, not connected with the Society, marked an advance in the liturgical movement. This was the Liturgical Week held in Birmingham from 28 to 31 October.[16] It was organised by the 'Birmingham Archdiocesan Liturgical Commission', a fact worth recalling. It must have been the first and perhaps the only liturgical commission of its time and for long afterwards. The programme was extensive, covering not only the Mass but the Divine Office and including some attention to the Eastern Liturgies in the shape of two lectures. Each day began with a pontifical Mass, at which the congregations in different churches sang the Ordinary from the *Kyriale* (no. IX and, on a feria, no. XVIII). The Proper was sung in full by students from Oscott and Capuchin friars from Olton. The report continues: 'After the Gospel the Archbishop [Williams] delivered an admirable discourse of the meaning of liturgical worship and the elements which the Church makes use of in associating her worship with that of Christ our Head, forms of prayer, ritual ceremonial and sacred music'.[17] The order of considerations is interesting and shows that liturgical notions had been making their way.

In addition to the liturgical celebrations there were lectures, one by Ernest Oldmeadow of the *Tablet* on 'The Liturgy and the Layman'. There was a performance of polyphonic music at the Oratory, which, as the reporter remarks, was properly called an *Oratorio*. Three 'Little Eucharistic Plays', written by C.C. Martindale SJ, were performed by children of the city with active participation (as allowed for by the texts) from the audience. The congress ended with the singing of the First Vespers of All Saints in St Chad's Cathedral on the evening of 31 October. In a very generous appreciation of the event in *Music and Liturgy*, Dom Dominic Willson compares it to similar events then taking place in France and Belgium. It is surely a pity that it was not repeated.

Taking a modest part in the congress was the Society of the Magnificat, founded in Birmingham in 1928 by Miss Kathleen Pond. Its main rule, the recitation of one of the canonical hours a day, was a simple device to secure some participation of the laity in the prayer of the Church. It attracted members from many parts of England and abroad; it organized courses of lectures and celebrations of the liturgy; and from 1935 published a quarterly, already referred to, called *Magnificat*. It carried articles by a great variety of writers and over the years explored many aspects of the liturgy that were not treated elsewhere.

The coming of Arthur Hinsley to Westminster as its archbishop in 1935 made possible a further venture that brought the Society of St

Gregory a good deal of public notice. Dom Bernard was quickly attracted to this man of broad views and generous sympathies. A friendship grew up between these two very different men and out of this relationship came the proposals made by the Cardinal for a Mass for Peace to be celebrated in Westminster Cathedral. The Society was to organize it and this, with the help of Fr Desmond Coffey and Fr Alec Robertson, it did. In three successive years, 1937-39, these Masses were celebrated in the cathedral and drew great crowds, estimated at 2,000, 'filling nave, aisles and galleries to capacity'. Under the direction of Dom Bernard the whole congregation sang the Ordinary of the Mass in plainsong and a schola of men (under the direction of Desmond Coffey) sang the Proper which Fr Robertson accompanied at the organ. As a reporter wrote: 'The vast Cathedral echoed to a volume of vocal music hitherto unheard within its walls'.[18]

These were occasions of some importance, showing what *could* be done (even if it was something of a *tour de force*) and revealing that the work of the Society had not been in vain. There can be no doubt, however, that the mood of the country, which desperately desired peace, and the encouragement of the Cardinal, greatly contributed to the success of these events.

Then in September 1939 came the war and with it the scattering of populations, the at-least partial disorganization of parish life and a rigidly enforced black-out that affected worship, especially the evening services. In the autumn and winter of 1940 the bombing of the cities and industrial centres created chaos and sometimes drove liturgical celebrations literally underground.

Notes

1 Described elsewhere—cf. p. 47.

2 As Fr S.J. Gosling once said after an illness, when he had attended Mass at a parish church, 'Father So-and-So preached the notices with great eloquence'.

3 This at least is the date as I can gather it from J.G. Vance and J.W. Fortescue, *Adrian Fortescue*: A Memoir, 1924, p. 55. For some reason the book does not appear in the bibliography nor in 'Some Biographical Dates and Facts'. There it is said that Fortescue 'revised' the English Missal for the Burns and Oates 'new' edition. What was the old one, and was Fortescue revising an older edition by someone else?

4 To be honest, it should be said that the battle was never fully won; and one reason for the unease felt in the catechetical changes in the 1950s and 1960s was that the work of Drinkwater had been too largely ignored.

5 Information about the origins both of the Conference and of the Summer School is now hard to come by, and it will have been observed that the above

account is somewhat tentative. I am, however, much indebted for information to Fr Robert Murray SJ, who kindly had certain passages from *The Month* 137, Jan.-June 1921, 142, July-Dec. 1923, photocopied for me. I have the impression that the scripture scholar Fr Cuthbert Lattey SJ had much to do with the foundation of the Summer School.

6   I am grateful to the authorities of Plater College for making available to me J.M. Cleary's *Catholic Social Action in Britain 1909-1959* which gives a complete account of the Guild and the College. From this book it also appears that there was contact with the Catholic social movement in Europe—one of the very few contacts between the English community and the Continent at the time.

7   It was inspired by Fr Martin D'Arcy SJ who collected a great number of pictures, vestments and other things that made Campion Hall something of a jewel-box.

8   Bourne's attitude at least in the 1920s, which was more *nuancé*, can be gathered from R.J. Lahey's essay 'Cardinal Bourne and the Malines Conversations' in *Bishops and Writers* (ed. Adrian Hastings), 1977.

9   *Ronald Knox*, 1959, p. 253.

10 Quigley's book was devotional and rubrical.

11 See p. 49.

12 Years later, a translation by the monks of St John's Abbey, Collegeville, Minnesota, appeared from their press.

13 See Alberic Stacpoole OSB. *Ampleforth Journal*, Autumn 1972 (Vol. LXXVII, iii), pp. 88-9.

14 They were re-worded in August 1971 to include them. See *Life and Worship*, January 1973 (inside cover).

15 *Ampleforth Journal, art. cit.*, p. 93. Although this is true, he did in fact set a very high standard—some thought too high—for congregational singing; and he (with others) was not always aware of the difficulty of plainchant for those who were unaccustomed to it.

16 Cf. *Music and Liturgy* (January 1936, p.82), where it is so described, though evidently the congress lasted only four days.

17 *Art. cit.*, p. 83.

18 The two above quotations are taken from *Ampleforth Journal, art. cit.*, p. 92.

3 English Liturgical Music before Vatican II

John Ainslie

It takes a little effort now, as we approach 1980, to step backwards in time to the 1950s—and a rather greater effort, impossible for most of us, to place ourselves in the 1930s or earlier. Before reviewing the scene of liturgical music in what now seem strangely halcyon days, it is well to remind ourselves—with or without nostalgia—of the setting in which liturgical music of the period was sung.[1]

There was the mid-morning 'Sung Mass'. From parish to parish, this might vary from a Low Mass, in which the choir and perhaps the people sang the *Missa de Angelis* while the priest 'got on with it', to the *Missa Cantata* (or, more rarely, Solemn Mass with deacon and sub-deacon) in which a full musical programme of Ordinary, Proper and ministers' chants was *de rigueur*, not to mention the *Asperges* or *Vidi aquam* at the beginning and the prayer for the king (in Latin, of course) at the end. Simple or elaborate as the music might be, the texts and ritual by which it was performed were exactly determined: only the more ambitious choir might venture beyond the prescribed order by launching into a motet of its choice at the Offertory or Communion.

If we are inclined to smile knowingly in the recollection that the congregation took little if any vocal part in these proceedings and no sacramental part (the early morning Mass was the 'Communion Mass' on account of the 'fasting from midnight' ruling), we should remind ourselves that the Solemn or High Mass—an essentially sung liturgy—was the standard form of the Roman Rite. Even if there were many people and places for whom a full *Missa Cantata*, let alone a Solemn High Mass, was a rarity, the ethos of solemnity, ceremonial and sacredness that went with it was a universal part of Catholic heritage and fostered a particular devotion *to* the Mass. The fact that most of the congregation at any Mass said their own private prayers during it does not detract from their awareness that here was a particularly sacred moment in which to say them. Its ethos of awe and mystery served to persuade them that it was perfectly appropriate to leave the priest and his servers to perform the sacred ritual with their backs to them at the east end while the choir looked after its appointed part from the west-end gallery. A further persuasion to the same effect at any Mass with singing was the difficulty of following both priest and choir at once, for they might well be uttering different texts at the same time—for instance, the Introit and/or Kyrie would be sung by the choir while the priest and MC would be saying the prayers at the foot of the altar (Ps 42 and the *Confiteor*): the dilemma was later increased when the advent of Dialogue Mass brought the Latin responses within the congregation's repertoire and competence. Thus did tradition and ethos together militate against congregational singing of liturgical music.

Yet Catholic congregations could and did sing—at Evening Service. Admittedly, numbers were very much smaller than the Sunday morning congregations and were dwindling long before the competition provided by Evening Masses on the one hand and television on the other. Those who came could certainly be termed 'devotees', but their silence in the morning would be largely compensated for by the quantity of vocal utterance, spoken and sung, that formed the order of Evening Service. Rosary, novenas and litanies were the common basis of that order—so were hymns: and even if the parish never had a sung Mass, it was never without its weekly Benediction in which the singing of the *O Salutaris* and *Tantum Ergo* was a necessary and enjoyable part. Few parishes might boast the complete repertory of 48 tunes for each of these hymns to be found in Tozer's *Benediction Manual* of 1898, still on sale in the 1960s; but few would be without this *vade mecum* of the parish organist or without an adequate variety of tunes for these hymns, which the people would sing with great fervour if little understanding. Moreover, many of the tunes were drawn from English sources and therefore stood alongside 'Soul of my Saviour' and 'Sweet Sacrament divine' as witnesses to the revival of a particularly English popular Catholic devotion in the nineteenth century.

The same spirit of devotion was evident when, at the end of Benediction or at other times during the Evening Service, the congregation rose to its feet and sang other hymns: 'Hail, Queen of heav'n, the ocean star' or 'Sweet Heart of Jesus, fount of love and mercy'. Even if one of Fr Vaughan's translations of St Alphonsus's hymns or Cardinal Wiseman's 'Full in the panting heart of Rome' might lead one's thoughts elsewhere, Fr Faber's 'Faith of our Fathers' sounded a particularly national note ('Mary's prayers shall win our country back to thee... '); though he would have been very surprised to see it in a somewhat amended form in both the *Methodist Hymn Book* and the *Baptist Hymnal*. There was scarcely any concession to the large proportion of Irish people in any English Catholic congregation: 'Hail, glorious Saint Patrick' came and went once a year but otherwise Irish music was never heard—the tune *Slane* for 'Be thou my vision' arrived after the Vatican Council from Anglican sources and *St Patrick's Breastplate* ('I bind unto myself today the strong name of the Trinity') is still to establish itself. The vast majority of the composers and authors whose names appeared in the *Crown of Jesus Hymn Book* of 1861 and in the first edition of the *Westminster Hymnal* (1912) were English. It was, of course, unfortunate that the mid-nineteenth century saw the nadir of English hymnody, but popular taste is an enigmatic creature, and the writer remembers his home parish in the 1950s when the 1912 edition of the *Westminster Hymnal*, though long displaced elsewhere by the revised edition of 1939, was still in use, and occasionally supplemented by choice pieces of Victorian sentiment harking back to the *Crown of Jesus* collection.

There was, then, a clear distinction between liturgical music and popular religious music; if the principal purpose of this chapter is to chart the progress of the former, it must be seen against the background of popular devotion with which it contrasted.

For all the professed loyalty of the Catholic community to the Holy See, not least in the wake of Pius X's draconian measures against Modernism, the attention it gave to his *Motu proprio, Tra le sollecitudini* of 1903, was minimal. True, Richard Terry took the matter of authenticity to heart and, to improve musical standards, began his editions, known as the 'Downside Masses', of sixteenth-century polyphony. This work was continued, with greater accuracy and success, by others, notably H.B. Collins (one of the first members of the Society of St Gregory) of the Birmingham Oratory. This kind of music soon began to be heard in many Anglican cathedrals and other great churches. Many indeed of the compositions and editions available hitherto had been eminently forgettable: Cary's turn-of-the-century list at the back of Tozer's *Benediction Manual* lists 71 settings of the Mass, mostly SATB, by such men as Alphonse Cary, Ch. Gounod, Oberhoffer, C.H. Rinck, Dom Gregory Ould of Fort Augustus, with pride of place given to the four Masses of Dom J. Egbert Turner of Ampleforth. Some of these were still to be heard as late as the 1970s; and if they are now dead, buried and scorned, they had their own charm and, in some cases, a much better musical construction than many a modern vernacular offering.[2]

Pius X's injunctions concerning the fostering of congregational music went largely unheeded, as did his exhortations on the cultivation of better plainsong and polyphony among choirs. There were many parishes in England where neither of these forms cf music was practised and many where they were not known at all. There were few teachers equipped to teach them—very few in the case of the chant—and few choirs, whether of men and boys or mixed, which could count on three or four good readers to make feasible the performance of the simplest piece of polyphony. For all the nostalgia for the beautiful singing of the past, there were far too many parishes where the music of the liturgy, even if rubrically correct, was far from beautiful. In some places the *Missa de Angelis* and *Credo* III had become established, though not necessarily as congregational music. Even then the rendering was often corrupted by what Laurence Bévenot calls 'lascivious semitones'. By rubric, the Proper of the Mass had to be sung, but often was not; and most parishes resorted to a simple psalm-tone or monotone—functional but hardly inspiring. If there were some parishes that could boast of a fine liturgical tradition, there were many that could make no such pretention (*plus ça change?*). Invincible ignorance or clerical *laissez-faire*?

By 1928 it could be said that liturgical practice and church music in parishes had reached a state of stagnation. Westminster Cathedral continued its tradition, monasteries and seminaries were singing plainchant and a little polyphony, but all this seems to have had little or no effect on worship as ordinary Catholics experienced it. It was a situation that needed new leadership and a new impetus. The leadership came from Dom Bernard McElligott, whose letter to the *Universe* in November 1928 resulted in the inaugural meeting of the Society of St Gregory of 12 March 1929.[3] There and then the four aims of the Society were laid down: they were both ideal and practical:

1. To maintain the dignity of the Sacred Liturgy as the supreme instrument of congregational worship.

2. To carry out the wishes of the Church with regard to church music; that is, to put into practice the instructions given by Pope Pius X in his 'Motu Proprio' on church music of 22 November 1903 and confirmed by Pope Pius XI in his Apostolic Constitution of 28 December 1928 on the same subject.

3. To provide each year a course of instruction in plainsong and polyphony for Catholic choirmasters, teachers and others practically interested.

4. To attempt, by mutual help, to find a solution for the practical problems of members.

The same gathering also decided to hold a Summer School of three days' duration at Blackfriars, Oxford, and in the following August this duly took place. Something of the atmosphere of this first meeting and the hopes it raised is suggested by one who was present: 'All seemed to enjoy themselves and to feel that here at last they had found something tangible.... Then passed for many of them that feeling of loneliness and depression, the consequence of many years of uphill fighting in their own places far removed from others with similar aims. They had found at Oxford new friends, new hopes and a fresh fount of inspiration in the person of their leaders, Fr McElligott and Fr Burke.'[4] Approval of the new society came with the Apostolic Blessing sent by Pope Pius XI himself.

Dom Bernard had evidently been making preparations before the Summer School with his brother monks at Ampleforth, for Dom Laurence Bévenot recalls that 'the demonstration of plainsong sung by four Ampleforth monks came as an utter eye-opener to many of the musicians attending'. Nevertheless the First Aim was the first aim: it was to be music for congregational worship in the liturgy, not music for its own sake.

The new impetus came from Pius XI—a pope not notoriously interested in liturgical matters—with the promulgation on 28 December 1928 of his Apostolic Constitution, *Divini Cultus*, which thus upgraded the *Motu proprio* and repeated with some force the injunctions of his predecessor. Significantly, it acknowledges that Pius X's exhortations had gone largely unheeded in many places and provides practical recommendations on putting them into effect. The clergy are to be properly instructed in Gregorian chant and sacred music, especially in seminaries, and are themselves to pass on this knowledge to their people either directly or through qualified teachers, 'as being matters closely associated with christian doctrine'. In phrases that re-echoed the *Motu proprio*, and that appeared much later in the Constitution on the Liturgy, the Pope states that 'the faithful come to church in order to derive piety from its chief source, by taking an active part in the venerated mysteries and public solemn prayers of the Church.... In order that the faithful may more actively participate in divine worship, let them be made once more to sing the Gregorian chant, so far as it belongs to them to take part in it.' This task will also be assisted by the work of societies striving to reform sacred music 'under the control of the ecclesiastical authorities'.

This letter came between the publication of Dom Bernard's letter to the *Universe* and the meeting at Ealing in 1929, but if he had been looking for an endorsement from the highest quarter he could not have received anything so clear and urgent as the *Divini Cultus*. The Gregorian chant is to be the instrument of congregational worship, and he never forgot that, and active participation in 'the divine mysteries' is the chief source of Christian piety, a theme that he elaborated over the years. In any appeal to authority for the support of his work, and that of the liturgical movement as whole, the *Motu proprio* and the Apostolic Constitution were the only two papal pronouncements on the subject until the appearance of *Mediator Dei* in 1947. These facts need to be kept in mind in judging the policy of the Society in the 1930s.

Another project that came very shortly after the foundation of the Society and that greatly assisted its work as well as the cause of plainsong is to be attributed to Dom Dominic Willson, a founder member of the Society, a good musician and an intelligent liturgist. He was already organist at Ampleforth when Dom Bernard McElligott was appointed choirmaster there in 1915. By 1929, Dom Willson was engaged in parish work at St Anne's, Liverpool, and he had come to see the need for a short book of simple plainsong which would make it available for congregational use in a more practical and popular manner than the existing *Kyriale*, which was restricted to the Ordinary of the Mass. Apart from this, the only other editions of plainsong available had been the complete volumes, the *Graduale Romanum* and the *Liber Usualis*, quite beyond the resources and competence of even reasonably accomplished choirs. His parish experience at St Anne's, Liverpool, not only suggested to him that such a simple publication should contain plainsong hymns and motets for use at Evening Service—thus capitalizing on the tradition of singing already established for that occasion—but also that he should place the book in the hands of the next generation of parishioners. So the idea of *Plainsong for Schools* was born. Part I, published in 1933, contained a selection of Ordinaries of the Mass and part of the Requiem Mass; but over one-third of the book was devoted to settings of the *O Salutaris* and *Tantum ergo* and hymns for the liturgical seasons for use at Evening Service, including (hopefully) Vespers.[5] The book was, in effect, a co-production by Rushworth and Dreaper of Liverpool and Desclée of Tournai; the preface of Part II, dated October 1934, claimed that in eighteen months over 100,000 copies of Part I had been sold—a remarkable feat by the standards of current hymn-book sales. Part II maintained the same balance between music for strictly liturgical use (the Proper of the Mass for the eight most important festivals of the year, including Forty Hours, plus Sunday Vespers) and plainsong intended for popular use at Evening Service (more settings of Benediction and Office hymns). It is doubtful whether the plainsong intended for use at 'devotions' ever became really popular, even though some of the plainsong tunes for the Benediction hymns did enter the repertoire of some parishes. The principal use of *Plainsong for Schools* in practice was for the Ordinary of the Mass: once its success had been proved, the way was clear for Cary's to produce its cards containing the plainsong of the Ordinary in modern notation for more widespread congregational use.

Of course, it takes more than a book to launch a movement. From the word 'go', the Society of St Gregory had met with considerable success, as witnessed by the Foreword which Archbishop Downey wrote in July 1930 for *Plainsong for Schools*, little over a year from the foundation of the Society:

> Here in Liverpool, and, I am told, also in Birmingham, Cardiff and Nottingham, many people have been converted to the Plain Chant movement by the simple lessons and practical demonstrations given by members of the Society of St Gregory.... It has been gratifying to see the way in which the music of the Church has been appreciated by those who have taken the trouble to master its principles and method. Like the Liturgy, it is in itself a prayer, an act of worship.

How was it done? By good leadership in rehearsal and during the Mass by a cantor who was also the congregational conductor—usually a priest, often a monk, who would explain the point of singing the liturgy as well as the way of doing so. In addition, the choir was given a challenge to meet in the singing of the Proper of the Mass according to its ability. (One may note in passing that the same method could well be used, *mutatis mutandis*, to promote liturgical music today.)

The competitive spirit between choirs as they became more proficient at singing the chant was given scope at regional festivals: in 1931 Father Burke presented a cup to the Society to be awarded to the winning choir of a national plainsong festival. In October of that year 400 voices gathered at Sedgley Park College, Manchester; the host choir won the cup for that year as it did on a number of subsequent occasions. In February 1932 two members of the Society assembled five choirs to perform no less than thirty-five items from the plainsong repertoire. In the same year, at Corpus Christi, Liverpool, Dom Dominic Willson had 5,000 people singing the plainsong together—with the aid of a trumpeter, for it was an outdoor festival. There were similar outdoor festivals at Rochester and Canterbury; St George's Cathedral, Southwark, was a significant promoter of congregational plainsong. Similar festivals were held in the Westminster Cathedral Hall, and in 1935 there was a four-day congress at St Chad's Cathedral, Birmingham.[6]

Evidently these were special occasions, usually taking place at cathedrals and major centres. How much this affected smaller and more remote parishes is rather more difficult to assess, although sales of *Plainsong for Schools* and the number of people and choirs attending the festivals suggest that the effect was widespread. However, it would all depend on the musical ability of the local choirmaster to teach his choir and the willingness of the local parish priest to encourage his people. If modern experience is at all relevant, these must have been limiting factors. Many congregations, though willing to sing the *Missa de Angelis* led from the organ bench, would be happy to leave the choir to sing other plainsong, even if they knew the melodies themselves—the obvious exception would be the occasional parish which had no choir but an enthusiastic leader, which would develop its congregational singing precisely because there was no choir to relieve it of this task. Certainly, plainsong was taught to children, thanks to *Plainsong for Schools*, but it is difficult to imagine that children could effectively lead the vocal participation of a congregation in a large church without leadership from the pulpit. It can scarcely be imagined that lay persons would have been permitted to assume this pulpit role; even if the parish was blessed with an enthusiastic priest, the unpredictability of clergy movements from parish to parish could and did cut off a liturgical tradition in a parish almost overnight. Mary Heathcock recalls with gratitude the days of Canon W. R. O'Keeffe when he was parish priest of Stourbridge, where there was a men-and-boys choir in the sanctuary and a women's choir elsewhere in the church as well. The Sunday Sung Mass was preceded by Terce; the Ordinary was always plainsong, the Proper was either full plainsong or Tozer—and there was often Vespers as part of the Evening Service. Nevertheless, the standard of singing was not high and she recalls that when she attended a meeting in Birmingham to hear Dom Bernard McElligott, she thought that if her choir could be taught to sing like that then plainsong might have appealed to more of the congregation.... Canon O'Keeffe died in 1937, and evidently there then appeared one 'who knew not Joseph'; and 'there were some lean years after that' until another priest with some liturgical interest and musical ability was appointed — the late Fr Gerard Peuleve.

The prowess of a liturgically-minded parish (-priest) would not, however, be limited to the single mid-morning Sung Mass. Mary Heathcock's recollections of Stourbridge continue: 'Evening Service would end with Benediction, but the first part would vary: Sunday Vespers, Compline, Vespers in honour of Our Lady (all these in Latin); in English, the Sacred Heart service which included psalm 102, Vespers for the different seasons of the year, the Blessed Sacrament Guild service, devotions for the conversion of England (Guild of Our Lady of Ransom), various litanies and the rosary in October and May. Nor were processions confined to May and Corpus Christi: every month brought one for the Children of Mary (first Sunday), the men (second), Blessed Sacrament procession which included the women (third) and the children (fourth). At all these services the people were expected to sing—and they did.' Why is it that people never objected to such a multiplicity of often extremely complex services, but seemed to thrive on them, whereas any attempt to treat the liturgy in more recent times with similar imagination has met with so much resistance from many who look for a stereotyped product?

Congregational singing on such devotional occasions was doubtless 'popular' in every sense of the word. It is difficult to use the same word of congregational singing at the liturgy—nor is it easy to determine just how much of this lasted for very long.

It is true that among those who took a particular interest in the 'plainsong apostolate' were some who perceived the liturgical purpose behind it. This can be gleaned, for example, from the preface to the revised edition of the *Westminster Hymnal,* published in 1939:

> The encouragement which the Holy See has given to the development of the liturgical spirit among the laity was borne in mind in the choice of hymns. At the same time it is hoped that this new edition will be considered to include a truly representative selection of popular Catholic hymnology [*sic*].

Of course, the hymn book could not be used at Mass (even for its Latin contents), but the new awareness of the liturgy did result in the inclusion of many more office hymns, mostly in Ronald Knox's translations, and the expansion of the section of Latin hymns to include the Magnificat and proses like *Rorate caeli*, nearly all provided with their plainsong melodies harmonized by Dom Gregory Murray. Other alterations to the previous edition of the *Westminster Hymnal* were more tentative: 'The Committee considered that there was no objection in principle to the occasional use of a non-Catholic translation when this possessed outstanding merit' must be compared with the triumphant words with which the words of the then Bishop David Mathew conclude the Preface: 'Native and redolent of the soil, yet so influenced in their style by changing taste, there was one factor

constant in these writers. Serene or didactic, unflinching or flam-
boyant, they were all faithful to the See of Rome.'

Even within the Society of St Gregory, the liturgical motive was not
always in the forefront: the issues of *Music and Liturgy* in the 1930s
bear witness to a long-running argument over the authenticity of the
Solesmes interpretation of the ancient plainsong manuscripts (which
broke out again in the early 1960s, but not within the ambit of the
Society); in a more peaceable vein, there were recondite articles on
minutiae, such as one entitled 'The Quilisma, its haunts and habits'.
The matter of interpretation was settled in favour of Solesmes but two
other problems came home to roost. One was a matter of practicality.
While it had been convincingly shown that the Ordinary of the Mass,
at least in the simpler plainsong settings, was within the competence
of a congregation if it was properly instructed and directed—qualifica-
tions which could not, however, be taken for granted—there was little
to aid the choir in tackling the Proper of the Mass. Cary had published
in 1933 a book containing the Proper chants of the Mass, set to psalm-
tones by Carlo Rossini, but there is no evidence that the Society of St
Gregory took any notice of it. When Laurence Bévenot offered a
similar script, set rather more imaginatively but equally simply to
melodies of his own, it was rejected by the Society—even though he
was a leading member of it. It was nevertheless published in 1944 and
achieved a respectable success.

The pursuit of plainsong and polyphony within a rather restricted
purview served to straitjacket the Society of St Gregory in the years
following the Second World War. But in fact there were movements in
another direction from 1940 onwards. The peripatetic apostolate of
courses and festivals of plainsong had come to an end with the declar-
ation of war (even though Summer Schools were held in 1942, 1943
and 1945); thereafter, under the editorship of Fr Joseph Connelly, the
Society's journal widened its interest to become principally concerned
with pastoral liturgy rather than music *per se*, a development reflected
in the change of name in 1944 from *Music and Liturgy* to simply
Liturgy, a policy continued by his successor as editor, Fr J. D.
Crichton. There were, however, some members who wished to have
scope for wider musical interests in the Church but who felt unable to
realize this within the leadership of the Society of that time: this group
formed itself into the Church Music Association of the Society of St
Gregory, and began an independent existence in 1955, although
friendly relations were maintained through a representative of each
organization being an ex-officio member of the executive body of the
other. In 1951, Dom Bernard McElligott had stepped down from the

executive leadership of the Society which was then assumed by Fr Joseph Connelly. The opportunities afforded to Dom Bernard and his assistants in pre-war years in terms of time and facilities were not repeated until John Michael East's directorship of the Church Music Association in 1968, of which more elsewhere. This inevitably restricted the outreach of the Society in its efforts to promote liturgical participation by means of plainsong, other than through its annual Summer School. It is perhaps significant of its impact in its early days that it is remembered by many to this day as the promoter of good plainsong rather than as promoter of liturgical participation.

There was one particular new initiative in 1954 which, like the Society of St Gregory Summer School in recent years, has contributed to the development of new liturgical music in Britain: the Spode House Easter Music Week. This at once became an annual event which has attracted some of the best musicians to discuss their approach to liturgical music and to create it afresh. George Malcolm and Fr Crichton addressed the first gathering, when Anthony Milner and Fr Sebastian Bullough OP were commissioned to prepare a translation and setting of English Vespers, which was duly performed the following year. Since then, it has not looked back and it is a thousand pities that its work has not been given a wider audience or a greater measure of integration with the work of the other organizations pursuing the same end. This may be because of its rather restricted view of the relationship between the trained, professional musician and the liturgical musician—an area in which much work still needs to be done. Elsewhere the situation was rather bleaker: indeed, if congregational singing of plainsong was widespread before the war, we have to conclude that between 1939 and the mid-1950s there was actually a decline in such singing. Despite the appearance of Dom Gregory Murray's *People's Mass* in 1950s—surely the most instantly singable setting ever composed, however one may assess its musical qualities—and of Laurence Bévenot's settings a few years later, all written with the English parish congregation specifically in mind, there are repeated pleas of despair at the reluctance of congregations to sing at Mass. Even the permission granted by *Mediator Dei*, confirmed and extended by the 1955 decree *Musicae sacrae disciplina*, whereby popular hymns could be sung in the vernacular at Low Mass, had no discernible effect on parish congregations, for whom the Sung Mass was a sung Mass and the Low Mass was not. Only in schools was this facility—and that granted by the 1958 Instruction to sing parts of the Ordinary or Proper plainsong at a Low Mass—used to some advantage. Sunday Sung Mass congregations continued to be happy to leave the singing to the choir, and the better the tradition of choral singing, the more silent the congregation became, even when something as familiar as the *Missa de Angelis* was performed. Moreover, some priests noted that numbers attending the Sung Mass were actually diminishing in favour of the Low Masses.

Choirs did not suffer the same problems—indeed, where there was adequate musical leadership their musical standards improved. For most people, then as now, 'sacred music' conjured up the image of polyphonic singing by lay choirs or plainsong sung by monastic choirs. With rare exceptions, choirs which desired to extend their repertoire tended to move towards polyphony rather than plainsong, not least because the polyphonic motet offered more freedom in the choice of texts (without much regard for liturgical propriety) and its more modern notation and technique was more accessible than plainsong for choir director and member alike. Indeed, some Catholic Church choirs achieved considerable fame during the 1950s and attracted the attention of reowned composers: Edmund Rubbra's *Missa in honorem Sancti Dominici* (1949) was followed by his *Missa à 3* of 1958, both for liturgical use and the latter dedicated to Henry Washington (of Brompton Oratory) and the Church Music Association of the Society of St Gregory. Similarly, George Malcolm's outstanding work at Westminster Cathedral attracted Benjamin Britten's *Missa Brevis* of 1959, composed especially for the Westminster Cathedral choir, and Lennox Berkeley's setting under the same title in the following year, both designed for use in the liturgy.

It is evidently a contentious question to ask how much such music involved the congregational audience in the liturgical action. By now we have learnt that active congregational participation does not require non-stop utterance. But in that these Mass-settings were scored for choir alone and took place in a liturgy in which the people made no vocal utterance whatever and where priests, ministers and choir were all at a distance from the congregation, it was certainly very different from the aims that Dom Bernard McElligott had stood for and attempted to achieve 25 years previously. Fr J. C. Buckley asked in the pages of *Church Music* in 1959: 'Have we understood the meaning of the liturgical movement or have we been too exclusively concerned with mere aesthetics and polished performances?'

Though some choirmasters and a small proportion of the clergy wrung their hands at their inability to get their congregations to sing, what none of them were able to do then (and we are learning the same lesson again twenty years later) is to lead the congregation as *animateur du chant*—even though the 1958 Instruction encouraged the use of a 'commentator' for this very purpose. The choirmaster was usually the organist and therefore tied to the keyboard, and there were few priests who had the know-how, liturgical or musical, to both inspire their people to sing and lead them in song. English people *will* sing when there is an occasion to warrant it. Arthur Oldham, in his *Missa Beatae Mariae Virginis*, written for the Spode Easter Week course in 1960, was one of the few church musicians on this side of the channel to appreciate the point of Joseph Gelineau's *Messe Responsoriale* of 1953, in which choir and congregation were both involved in an integrated structure. Now, in 1978, so many Mass-settings later, it seems that we still have to learn how to incorporate priest, cantor, choir and congregation in a unit of liturgical music which will unite them in worship—readers who know something of Bernard Huijbers's compositions will catch a glimpse of what is still to be realized.

Notes

1   The writer is particularly indebted to Dom Laurence Bévenot and Geoffrey Boulton Smith for their assistance in providing recollections and documentary material for this chapter.

2   For a different view, see Nicholas Kenyon, below, p. 134.

3   For further details, see pp. 41 – 2 above.

4   *Ampleforth Journal*, Autumn 1972 (Vol. LXXVII, iii), p. 89. Fr John Burke was Dean of University College, Dublin, and even at that early date was Vice-president of the Society. There are many priests and lay-people who have attended the Society's summer schools in the intervening fifty years who have found in them similar enjoyment and inspiration against a similar background of depression in their own parishes.

5   Responsible for the selection of part of the content, and also the author of the introduction, was Dame Laurentia McLachlan, Abbess of Stanbrook. A distinguished member of the Society of St Gregory, she was for many years one of England's leading proponents and scholars of plainchant, with many publications to her credit.

6   For further details, see above, p. 44.

4 The liturgical Movement from 1940 to Vatican II

J. D. Crichton

The war that broke out in 1939 affected the life of the whole population more deeply than any previous war. Younger people were gradually absorbed into the armed forces, and industry had to be organized for a total war production. Vast numbers of people were sent here
and there to the most improbable parts of the United Kingdom and
indeed of the world, and the rest of the able-bodied had to work long
hours in shifts that paid no respect to Sunday. In addition, hundreds
of thousands had to give whatever time was left over to fire-fighting,
to ambulance work and to the care of the victims of aerial bombardment. Families were at least temporarily broken up by the (necessary)
evacuation procedures that sent children far from their homes. There
were indeed the eight or so months of the 'phoney' war when little
happened in England, though Hitler meanwhile occupied the greater
part of Europe. In June 1940 there was the retreat from Dunkirk, and
in August and September the Battle of Britain. All through the
autumn until Christmas there was the bombardment of the greater
cities, and for millions life became barely endurable. The bombing
continued with slowly decreasing momentum throughout 1941 and
then, in the last years of the war, London and the South East suffered
from the unpredictable 'doodle-bugs' that caused considerable dam-
age and loss of life at a time when people were tiring and deprived of
nourishing food.

The war years

In such circumstances worship became very difficult and it might be
thought that the liturgical movement would have been killed.
Strangely enough this was not so. Some at least of the chaplains to the
armed forces had been touched by the liturgical movement, and when
they had to minister to large numbers of young men and women they
realised the possibilities of a communal celebration of the Mass which
usually took the form of the Dialogue Mass, in Latin of course. A
special edition of the *Simple Prayer Book*, distributed widely to the

forces, became an instrument for the promotion of the Dialogue Mass in which the congregation usually made the responses of the server and recited the *Gloria in excelsis*, the Creed, the *Sanctus* and the *Agnus Dei* in Latin with the celebrant. An example of what could be done is the work of Fr Clifford Howell SJ, who joined up as a chaplain and within two weeks was in France. Because, as he says, he was in a country where the Dialogue Mass was permitted (and indeed encouraged) he trained his men to take part in such Masses with the help of the *Simple Prayer Book*. This practice spread to other units, was taken up by the RAF and was 'pretty usual among all the armed forces abroad'. It is highly probable that this influenced practice at home; for, after the retreat from Dunkirk, chaplains and men returned home and either in camps or in parish churches continued their practice of the Dialogue Mass. Some chaplains got 'ticked off', and in some dioceses the Dialogue Mass was forbidden altogether.[1]

Such were the complexities of the liturgy at the time, which at least by the celebrant had to be said wholly in Latin, that considerable ingenuity had to be exercised to help people to understand and participate in the Mass. In England it was not generally realised, as it was (at least after the war) in France, Germany and Belgium, that a lay-reader might be used to read the Epistle and Gospel; and, as Fr Howell records, he had to train men to do this. In those days there was no question of women doing *anything* in the liturgy. To this form of Mass were eventually added hymns, though the corpus of hymns suitable for singing at Mass was very small. Thus the German formula, the *Betsingmesse* (the prayer-song Mass), known in German-speaking countries since at least the eighteenth century, came gradually into use in England. Rather later, Fr Howell organized all this in a booklet *Mass Together* which eventually had an enormous circulation. Here he introduced new and more suitable hymns, some written *ad hoc*, though usually set to well known tunes.

But this is to anticipate a little. It seems certain—though a good deal of research would be needed to establish the point—that the war acted as a catalyst on the Catholic community in Great Britain. There were vast numbers of young men and women in the armed forces and their Catholic Christianity was put to the test, sometimes severely. Thanks no doubt to improved religious education, especially in grammar and boarding schools, most of them seem to have stood the test well. They were well served by their chaplains who, of course, were for the most part young; and often there grew up an intimacy between chaplain and people that made possible discussion of the problems and concerns that were in the forefront of their minds. It can hardly be doubted that this produced a ferment of ideas that found expression in the last years of the war and in the years immediately afterwards.

In these years there were two factors that were of great importance for the Catholic community. One was the personality of Cardinal Hinsley who emerged as one of the greatest figures of the war. His radio addresses and sermons, in which he combined a strong patriotism with a profound grasp of Christian principles, made a deep impression. Over and over again he expressed the sense of the nation and it was not too difficult to draw together the spiritual forces of the nation. This found expression in the establishment of the Sword of the Spirit movement, promoted by the Cardinal and the Archbishop of Canterbury, for the exposition and upholding of Christian principles in national and international life. It was an event of some importance when the two prelates appeared on the same platform to be welcomed with rapturous applause by the audience. When together they recited the Lord's prayer, it seemed like an ecumenical breakthrough—though some canonists were not pleased! The Sword of the Spirit represented an exercise in what is now regarded as normal Christian collaboration: to work together for the promotion of what could be agreed on. Whatever the later vicissitudes of the movement—and they were not happy—it remains the first ecumenical endeavour in this country in modern times. Clergy and laity of different denominations learnt to work together, came to know each other, visited each other and began to listen to each other. Nor was this 'dialogue' confined to the 'high-ups'. Ordinary parish clergy as well as their people drew closer to their brethren in other churches, though the incidence of such encounters was patchy. Some Catholics were fearful and some clergy, both bishops and priests, were opposed. Nonetheless, the whole phenomenon showed that the Catholic community had moved from the fringe of national life to somewhere near its centre. This could not but have effects on the way Catholics spoke and wrote and behaved. One effect of this situation was to throw up new faces and new minds, people who had benefitted from the entrance of Catholics into the universities before the war. Not only were there the Woodruffs, the Hollises, the Dawsons but there was a Barbara Ward (now Lady Jackson) who on radio and in lectures to a variety of audiences revealed that there were Catholics who could bring forward new ideas and throw fresh light on social problems. With such people in the Catholic community it was improbable that the Church could relapse into its former social quietism. Nor did it. Discussion was active in many levels of life in the community, old views were being examined and new ideas considered on their merits. This practice of discussion would be carried forward in the years immediately after the war in the many conferences that took place, notably at Spode House in Staffordshire, the effect of whose work over some three decades has been to educate the laity (and often the clergy) towards a mature Catholicism.

English in the liturgy

Among the subjects discussed, none was more prolonged and at times more vehement than that concerning the use of the people's language in the liturgy. It began in the columns of the *Catholic Herald*, then edited in stimulating, (and some would say provocative) fashion by Count Michael de la Bedoyère. The controversy began, if I am not mistaken, with a statement made by Fr C.C. Martindale that, in an audience with Pius XI, the Pope had said that some use of the vernacular in the liturgy would be of advantage to the people. Thenceforth the controversy raged through the years and gradually invaded other papers, both periodical and weekly. Bombs might fall, troops go into France and the Navy blow U-boats out of the sea, but nothing could abate the eagerness of so many to urge their views either for or against the introduction of English into the liturgy. Nor was all this discussion mere crankiness. It was clear that many of the writers had grasped the essentials of liturgical, corporate worship and desired a change so that it could be in effect achieved. On the contrary, it would not be unfair to say that those who were opposed to the use of English in worship often showed a lamentable misunderstanding of it.

In any case, it was not all hot air and no action. In the summer of 1942 Fr S. J. Gosling, long in favour of the use of English in our worship, invited a number of priests who had shown interest (and had joined in the *Catholic Herald* controversy) to a meeting that convened at Stanbrook Abbey.[2] From this came the English Liturgy Society (later the Vernacular Society) whose purpose was to promote the cause of the use of the mother tongue in worship.[3] It had a rocky history. Bishops did not like it, and from time to time put obstacles in the way of the publication of its quarterly magazine. Eventually it was brought under the supervision of the Archbishop of Westminster, who appointed Canon Ronald Pilkington as its director. Nevertheless the campaign went on. Articles pro and contra appeared in *Liturgy* and *Magnificat* and eventually the Vernacular Society prodced a volume of collected essays on the subject, edited by C. R. A. Cunliffe (1956). It would be untrue to say that English Catholic society was split down the middle by the subject, for many chose not even to notice it; but among those concerned with the liturgy it did cause a certain division that was not wholly healed by the Second Vatican Council.

Whatever the merits of the cases put on one side or the other (and the whole controversy is now obsolete), the discussion revealed that among a great number of people there had been an advance in the understanding of the liturgy. Slow as England was in taking up new ideas (that were in fact very old), localized as various efforts for a better and more communal celebration had been, there had also been that dangerous thing, teaching. Not official teaching, but a general spread of ideas that were ventilated in weekly newspapers and periodicals as well as in some schools. By 1945 there were three liturgical societies, that of the Magnificat, the Vernacular Society and the Society of St Gregory. The last was the most important in that it enjoyed the patronage of the bishops and had a wider membership than any other. In the dark period of 1940-42 it underwent a certain change.

The progress of the Society of St Gregory

Hitherto it had been regarded as a society for the teaching of plainsong and to a lesser extent polyphony. After two years' intermission when its annual summer school could not meet on account of the bombings, the school of 1942 showed a change. To the lectures on plainsong and its practice were added lectures on the liturgy itself. What prompted this change is not quite certain, though it seems that interest in and teaching on the Church as the Mystical Body of Christ, which had had increasing emphasis in the years immediately before the war, had something to do with it. This influence was palpable in the Society in the next few years after Pius XII had issued his encyclical *Mystici Corporis* (1943; E.T. 1944) in which he stated that the eucharist is the culmination of the life of the Church and 'that (in the eucharist) the faithful are associated in the common prayer and supplication and, through the hands of the priest, whose voice alone renders the Immaculate Lamb present on the altar, they themselves offer to the Eternal Father this most pleasing Victim of praise and propitiation for the needs of the whole Church' (n. 81). Although five years later *Mediator Dei* would put the matter somewhat more adequately ('The rites and prayers of the Mass show no less clearly that the offering of the victim is made by the priest and people together' n. 91 (E.T.)), this was something to go on and was immediately made use of. The pattern that was adopted in 1942, instruction on the liturgy along with the teaching and singing of plainsong, has remained the same to the present day although the style and variety of music studied and used has changed beyond recognition. But through the institution of lecturers and the discussions that flowed from them, the Society became one of the chief forces in the country for the education of people in the meaning of the liturgy. It was also a factor that led to a continually increasing membership both of the Society[4] and the summer schools which maintained a steady figure of about one hundred and fifty, sometimes more, sometimes rather less. Originally always held at Oxford, from 1946 the summer schools were held in different places all over England (there was one in Scotland—Glasgow) in the hope—not always fulfilled—that the Society would reach people who otherwise did not know of its activities.

Until 1951 Dom Bernard McElligott remained the head of the Society, his official title being 'Vice-President', for in 1938 he had asked Cardinal Hinsley to be President, an invitation he graciously accepted.[5] In spite of a precarious health and a hesitant manner, Dom Bernard remained over the years in control of the Society and from time to time showed an openness to new ideas not always to be found among other members of the Society. He lectured frequently, not only at the summer schools but widely in England; he arranged regional meetings in different places at Easter and other times of the year; he tirelessly took rehearsals in plainsong until deteriorating health made the work impossible.

The other instrument of instruction was the Society's quarterly magazine, first called *Music and Liturgy*, then in 1944, reflecting the expansion of interests of the Society, simply *Liturgy* and finally (1970) *Life and Worship* in an effort to show that worship had to do with Christian living and vice versa.[6] It is instructive to look over the back numbers of the magazine, which from 1940 was edited by Fr Joseph Connelly of Oscott College until 1952 when the present writer took over. For some years Fr Connelly had been opening up the outlook of the magazine, and many of the questions of the day concerning liturgy were reflected in its pages. This policy was continued and the magazine became the means by which instruction in the meaning of the liturgy was given and movements on the continent of Europe and in the USA were made known. If one compares its articles with the subject-matter of the successive summer school lectures, it will be seen that hardly any question concerning liturgy that was authoritatively decided by the Second Vatican Council went undiscussed. It is not for those of us who were concerned with the work of the Society and the magazine to judge the value of our efforts, but perhaps we may be allowed the observation that the Society did what it could to prepare people for the reform of the liturgy that came with the Council.

The Society was not content simply to teach music at its summer schools or to instruct through the pages of *Liturgy*. In two different ways it reached out to a wider public. It did so first with a little book, *The Parish Mass Book*, compiled by a group of priest-members of the Society, which appeared in 1955. Its purpose was to secure an intelligent use of the Dialogue Mass whose pattern was not understood everywhere. Thus certain texts like the *Gloria* were printed in bold type and the preliminary psalm (which provided great practical difficulties) in smaller type. This was reinforced by an introduction indicating how the book should be used. The book went through six subsequent editions and two revisions, the last one in 1962 being the most extensive. By this time it had been arranged for three types of celebration: Dialogue Mass simply, Dialogue Mass with hymns (a selection of suitable ones was provided) and Sung Mass. Two sets of plainsong Masses were included. This little book had a wide circulation and it was reported that at one point no less than 50,000 copies had been sold.[7]

The second endeavour was the publication of two records, published by HMV in 1961, of plainsong Masses and other pieces. Its purpose was to show (yet again!) that ordinary congregations could sing selected plainsong texts and so take an active part in a conventional Sung Mass.[8]

However, one would not wish to give the impression that the Society was the only agent at work. One significant feature of post-war Catholicism was the quantity of publications on the subject of the liturgy. With the foundation of such firms as Blackfriars Publications, Darton, Longman and Todd, and Geoffrey Chapman, came the translation of a vast amount of literature on the liturgy. The names of Jungmann, Bouyer, Martimort, Roguet and many others appeared regularly in the publishers' lists. True, there was little enough native work, but members of the Society made a modest contribution with the publication of pamphlets (e.g. *Liturgy and the Layman* by the then Archbishop of Edinburgh) and small books like Canon A.S.E. Burrett's *We Celebrate our Redemption* and Fr Norman Swinton's *Liturgy in the Home* which included a list of somewhat recondite liturgical dishes. But the writer who made the most notable impact was Fr Clifford Howell. In 1953 he published (with the Catholic Social Guild) what might be called the first text-book in English on liturgy: *The Work of our Redemption*, which by 1975 had reached its fourth (revised) edition.[9] It was the fruit of his first visit to the USA in 1949 and of a series of articles which appeared in *Orate Fratres* (now *Worship*).

To help the parish clergy to present and celebrate the revised Holy Week liturgy of 1955 he had ready another book by 1956, *Preparing for Easter*, which has had a wide circulation and has run into several editions. In addition, he provided practical aids with his *Mass Together* (already mentioned) and an edition in English set to plainsong of *Sunday Compline*, which was widely used and much appreciated. This list could be extended, but it could be said to have come to a grand climax with his translation of the Constitution on the Liturgy which with great effort he had made available by the end of the second session of the Council which had just promulgated it.

The penetration of the parish

Probably however his most effective work was done through what he calls his 'invention' of the 'Liturgical Weeks'. These lasted from Sunday to Sunday, and on each day in the week there was instruction on various aspects of the liturgy based on the doctrine of the church as the Mystical Body of Christ. *Pari passu* went practical instruction in participation in the liturgy both by (Latin) dialogue and song leading gradually to full participation on the concluding Sunday. Encouraged by Canon McNarney, Fr (now Canon) W. Raftery, the two Backhouse brothers, William and Herbert, Mgr J. C. Buckley, names of parish priests which should not be forgotten, as well as others, he gave these 'weeks' all over the country and eventually in the USA and Australia. Again, it is difficult to gauge their effect, at least in England; but they were undoubtedly an extended education for a very large number of people in the meaning of the liturgy.

The educational factor

Another factor in the spread of liturgical notions and practice was the renewed and expanded Newman Association. This expansion bore witness to the increasing number of Catholics attending universities, an increase that gathered ever greater momentum in the decades before the Council. Through the universities and access to professional organizations the Catholic community began to develop an educated middle class on a scale unknown before the war. Here was a great stirring of ideas, and, both through the university chaplaincies and the regional and national meetings of the Association a new understanding of the liturgy grew along with an improved practice. In most if not all chaplaincies, Dialogue Mass was the order of the day, and 'active participation' was something that was soon taken for granted. Unfortunately, also, a generation-gap, which was at least partly an education-gap, developed between the parish clergy and these new laity with sharp, well-trained minds and an experience of worship that was very different from the humdrum celebrations of their parish churches. Still, up and down the country there were large numbers of people who wanted an improved liturgical practice and some saw the need for liturgical reform. Another result was that the quality of parish life began to change. An increasing number of articulate Catholics wished to have a greater say in the running of the church. In many places the old-fashioned 'good' Catholic for whom the parish priest's word was both the law and the gospel began to give way to people who made up their own minds, who were often ready to collaborate, but who were not content to be simply subordinates.

The grammar schools, the boarding schools and perhaps especially the convent schools, from all of which the new graduates were drawn, also promoted a more satisfactory liturgical practice, so that it could be said that very large numbers of Catholics had been initiated into a celebration of the liturgy that was often lacking in their parishes. Much the same could be said of the secondary schools, now usually with chapels of their own, where at least some priests and teachers encouraged community celebration. As the pages of past issues of *Liturgy* show, this too was often a cause of tension between the schools and the parish.

For those who experienced it at the time, the slowness of bishops and parish clergy to adopt practices that were in use in many places in Europe, and increasingly in the United States, was puzzling and exasperating. Of the Dialogue Mass, more than one bishop said that he would not allow it as it would disturb both the priest and the laity. Until 1958 (and probably later) such Masses were forbidden in six dioceses, allowed occasionally in four others, and given some encouragement in only three.[10] In these years after the war, when the Church was in rapid expansion, when priests and people often had to use makeshift buildings for worship, and when social habits were also changing, it is not improbable that liturgical practice suffered something of a setback. The retention of choirs and the maintenance of the Sung Mass became ever more difficult.

The influence of radio

Both before the war and during and after it, there was a good deal of religious broadcasting in which Catholics had a share, though a regular complaint was that that share was not big enough. In the late 1920s and early 1930s, Fr Martindale—with his electric utterance, clarity of thought and understanding of his invisible audience—had made a considerable impact. Martin D'Arcy, Ronald Knox and Bede Jarrett made less frequent but widely appreciated contributions. Church services were broadcast every Sunday, though little was done at this time to adapt the service to the medium: microphones were planted in the church and the service went forward without much regard for the listener at home. But things had been changing in the BBC, and by 1947 it was realised that church services had to be 'produced'. It was at this time (and not without some opposition) that Fr Agnellus Andrew OFM was appointed assistant to the religious department. With his coming, Catholic broadcasting began to take on a more professional air, and by his own enormous efforts the style and quality of Catholic broadcasting began to improve. His work over the years is yet to be assessed (for example, it is often forgotten that he was the first chairman of the Church Music Association of the Society of St Gregory and influential in its affairs for a number of years), but his contribution to better liturgical celebration is undeniable.

The impact of his work could be felt in three different areas: liturgical services, the conventional evening service, and others that did not fall into either category.

The broadcasting of the Mass before the Council presented considerable difficulties. The services was all in Latin, parts of it were silent, and its basic shape was not well known, even to some Catholics. In these circumstances, commentary had to be used, especially for the silent parts; and the Epistle and Gospel had to be 'read over'. Fortunately the Knox translation of the New Testament had become available as a permitted text and could replace the Douai Version which was not strong on communication. In spite of the difficulties, the Mass was broadcast successfully; and, in the process, priests and congregations as well as listeners learnt a good deal about it. Broadcasting also gave stimulus to an improved musical accompaniment to the Mass. The parish from which the broadcast came realised, in greater or lesser degree, that what was tolerable for home consumption was not necessarily good enough for a wider audience. Here, the work that had been done by the Society of St Gregory and other agencies began to show its value. Where circumstances were propitious—that is, where there was some active participation—plainsong settings made possible a celebration by the whole community. Preaching, too, benefitted from radio exposure. The preacher had to understand the medium he was using and to project his imagination to those who were not Catholics or not Christians at all.

As the Dialogue Mass with hymns came to be used more and more, this form of celebration also provided a medium suitable for broadcasting. At least after 1958, even lay-people were heard reading the lessons of the Mass on the radio.

It would not be too much to say that an improved understanding of the Mass and a better celebration of it were the result of many years of broadcasting.

Evening services presented a problem. The official prayer of the Church, Vespers and Compline, was in Latin; and this was unsuitable for the Sunday-night service, which was meant for the general public. Services of varying content were made up—some more successful than others— usually consisting of a reading from scripture, hymns, some prayers, of course the sermon, and Benediction in Latin—hence more commentary. It was probably in the matter of hymns that broadcasting brought about an improvement. The 1939 edition of the *Westminster Hymnal* was a distinct advance on the old one; it contained some distinguished verse, some of it translations (occasionally convoluted, it should be said) by Ronald Knox. Considerable care had been taken over the melodies and their arrangements, and the whole book in words and music was respectable. The rendering of hymns was also greatly improved, largely under the stimulus of Fr Agnellus himself, who did a great deal to get rid of what Bishop Mathew in the introduction to the *Westminster Hymnal* called 'the loud and draughty singing' which was the tradition among us. Not always so loud—and hymns were often sung incredibly slowly. Churches that had experience of broadcasting soon abandoned that tradition, though, alas, it continued elsewhere (and still does in some places).

The third category of services—for example, the People's Service on Sunday morning and the hymn-singing session on Sunday evening—provided other opportunities. The People's Service was really built up round the sermon, which was interspersed with hymns and perhaps readings and prayers. The hymn-singing benefitted from the processes described above, and in the hands of a skilled broadcaster like Canon M. McNarney (who had a remarkable success in this genre) the whole service could do much to bring the Gospel to the people. In the Sunday-evening service, which lasted for half-an-hour, a commentator spoke for a minute or so before each hymn; and again with care and thought a whole message could be delivered in a way that was rather outside the Catholic tradition of worship. Once again, the Westminster collection, though in some ways limited (it was short on 'praising' hymns), proved to be useful.

In this context, it may be remarked that Dom Bernard McElligott realised the potential of the medium, and in the 1940s was active in this field. Apart from his personal contributions, he arranged for either Vespers or Compline to be broadcast from the summer schools for a number of years. These broadcasts took their place alongside those of Evensong from Anglican cathedrals and other great churches on Tuesday afternoons.

It should not go unnoticed that the BBC was also instrumental in producing an ecumenical climate. Priests and laity not only worked with their Christian counterparts within the BBC but the regional boards for the discussion of religious programmes brought together clergy and laity of all denominations who found that they could work happily together. It was a valuable work that seems to have gone un-recognized.

The movement on the Continent

However reluctant the English clergy as a whole were to take account of what was happening in Europe, and however lukewarm to the suc-cessive measures of reform that came from Rome in this period, the liturgical movement was making progress. This is not the place even to sketch the vicissitudes of the liturgical movement that received a new impetus when, in the midst of a most horrible war, the French and German movements came together, largely through the energy of an Alsace parish priest, the Abbé Rauch. It is interesting to reflect, however, that at a time when there could have been no communica-tion between England and the Continent there was a similar ferment in England on liturgical matters, as has been said above, though the Franco-German movement was much more radical. Briefly, it put into currency the notion that the liturgy is for the people, that it must be made available to the people, and that every means must be used to bring this about. In a word, it must be rooted in the life-situation of the people. This kind of movement rapidly came to be known as a movement for a pastoral liturgy. Nonetheless, it was based on con-siderable scholarship, and in the conferences and congresses that began in 1950 scholars of many disciplines—exegetes, theologians, liturgists and even sociologists—worked vigorously together. French liturgical practice was widely transformed and by 1950 the Germans, who started from a better base, achieved a measure of participation in the celebration of the liturgy that was the envy of those foreigners who experienced it. A good deal of all this was reported, sometimes incorrectly, in the religious press; but it made little or no impression in England.

Then there were the liturgical congresses that had been held in Europe from 1950 onwards: Munich 1950, Maria-Laach 1951, St-Odile

(Alsace) 1952, Lugano 1953, Mont-César (Belgium) 1954, and Assisi in 1956 when there was something like 1,000 participants from almost every country in the world. The gatherings at Maria-Laach, St-Odile, Lugano and Assisi were reported in the pages of *Liturgy* and the last in those of the *Tablet* and the *Catholic Herald*. Their importance was that they considered in depth the nature of the liturgy, reviewed its current state in the light of pastoral needs, and gradually began to consider the need for reform. At Maria-Laach, Father Loew, a Redemptorist and a member of the Congregation of Rites, made it known that reasoned requests for reform, based on tradition, would receive due consideration in Rome. Thenceforth at the end of each congress 'conclusions' containing reasoned pleas for certain changes were drawn up and sent to Rome. The two gatherings at Lugano and Assisi respectively were the most important, the location of the former making possible the attendance of Roman officials, headed by Cardinal Ottaviani, and the latter because it was presided over by Cardinal Cicognani, Prefect of the Congregation of Rites. Not everything he heard there was to his liking, however, especially a strong plea for the use of the vernacular that was distributed among the participants by the Americans. It is worth recording that Fr Jungmann received a standing ovation before and after his lecture, and hardly less popular was Fr Bea, not yet a cardinal and known only as a scripture scholar who spoke on the Word of God. The presidency of the Prefect of the Congregation of Rites, and the concluding address given by Pius XII in Rome, gave the congress a semi-official status, and those who were involved in the liturgical movement could be forgiven if they thought that the official Church was with them.

In another field of activity there was the same reluctance to look ahead or even abroad. Partly as a result of the war, which had destroyed or seriously damaged many churches in Europe, and partly as the result of the movement of people after the war, the years between the end of the war and the Council saw a considerable number of new or restored churches being built. Reflection on the nature and function of church-building had been proceeding on the continent for many years before 1939, and new churches, expressing these insights, had been going up. After the war this process continued, especially in Germany, and many churches had been arranged for celebration *versus populum* though in England permission to do anything of the sort was refused. Churches built in England as late as the 1950s or early 1960s were obsolete by 1965. Cardinal Ottaviani, who once described himself as 'the policeman of the Church' (he was head of the Holy Office), could celebrate Mass facing the people in 1953 in a newly-designed church in Lugano. This could be and was reported in *Liturgy*, but the English people remained unmoved. In this, as in other matters, the English Channel proved to be an all-too-effective Water Curtain.

The Conference of Practical Liturgy

Even so, yet another attempt was made to propagate pastoral-liturgical notions. In an effort to reach a greater number of the pastoral clergy, the Conference of Practical Liturgy came into being in 1962. There were those who felt that, although the Society of St Gregory had done good work in studying through the years the central points of the liturgy, something more needed to be done. The number of priests attending the summer school had always been small; too many associated the Society with the teaching of plainsong. Yet many of the clergy were interested in pastoral liturgy; they wished to deepen their knowledge of the subject and find a platform for the discussion of their situations and difficulties. A group of priests, both academics and members of the pastoral clergy, met at Spode House, Staffordshire, early in 1962 to consider the setting up of a conference. As the first result, over 200 priests in the United Kingdom were circularized, asking if they felt the need for a pastoral liturgical conference. As the replies came in it soon became clear that a sufficient number did, and a conference was arranged for September. The subject chosen was baptism, to be considered theologically and in its pastoral context. In the event some sixty priests attended (a dozen or so being prevented at the last moment) and found the conference to their liking. They pressed that the conference should continue, that it should be held annually and at Spode House. Since the Warden, Fr Conrad Pepler, was keen and very welcoming, there was no difficulty at all about the last point. Conferences were held in successive years until 1968, though in the following year the response fell, partly because by this time diocesan gatherings for the clergy for the study of the (new) liturgy were being organised. In the six years of its existence the conference considered, as well as baptism, The Parish (1965), The Christian Sunday (1964), The Mass and the People of God (1966), the Ministry of the Word (1967), at which C. H. Dodd made a notable and most gracious contribution, and in 1968 Penance: Virtue and Sacrament. All the papers, except those on Baptism and the Christian Sunday, were published as books, and thus the second purpose of the conference, to provide literature on pastoral liturgy, then sadly lacking, was achieved.

The printed word

There was indeed a good deal of liturgical literature being published in the later years of the period, though much of it could not be described as pastoral. Mention however must be made of the English translation of J.A. Jungmann's great and in some ways epoch-making *The Mass of the Roman Rite* (New York, 1951, 1955) which in spite of its heavy annotation and not very attractive English was widely read. In 1960 came Charles Davis's *Liturgy and Doctrine* and in 1961 I.H. Dalmais's *Introduction to the Liturgy*, both of which explored and expounded the Christian mystery largely in the terms of Dom Odo Casel. These were backed up by the London edition of the latter's *The Mystery of Christian Worship* that appeared in 1962. A third edition (translated by H.E. Winstone) of Pius Parsch's popular *The Liturgy of the Mass* had appeared in 1957, and there was Amiot's little *History of the Mass*, a volume in the Faith and Fact series ably edited for the English-speaking world by Lancelot Sheppard. A Downside symposium on liturgy, held at le Bec-Hellouin in 1962, produced *True Worship* (1963), again edited by Lancelot Sheppard. There were others, notably Pius Parsch's *The Church's Year of Grace* (St John's Abbey, Collegeville, Minnesota, 1957) which in five volumes covered the whole of the liturgical year and which was a great stand-by for those priests who were concerned to preach from the liturgical texts. It will be apparent that most of these books were translations and that they appeared towards (or after) the end of our period. But they were the fruits of the pre-conciliar Church and bear witness to an ever-increasing interest in the liturgy (for publishers are not charitable institutions) that existed before the Council.

A rather different kind of writer whose work for the liturgy was continued thoughout the period should be commemorated here. This was Canon J. B. O'Connell. By 1941 he had made his name as a rubricist, first as editor and reviser of Fortescue's *Ceremonies of the Roman Rite described* (four revised editions), and then with his three-volume *The Celebration of Mass* (1941) which in intelligent fashion showed how the Roman rite of the time should be celebrated. But it was with his replies to queries in the *Clergy Review*, from 1953 onwards, that he began a different sort of campaign. Under the editorship of Charles Davis, what had been a clerical periodical became a review that appealed to a wider public, and the editor showed over the years an increasing concern for the liturgy. Articles on the word of God, a particularly powerful one written by the editor himself, in which probably for the first time in England he introduced the notion of the 'real presence' of Christ in the word in the liturgy, and on 'liturgical preaching' as well as others, appeared from time to time. But in his answers month by month, and especially after the Instruction of 1958, O'Connell was propagating the notion of a pastoral liturgy. A recognized expert on the Roman documents in this field, 'again and again, though always quietly, he insisted on what the Roman documents *allowed*... (and) over at least one point his views were not popular with some bishops. There was a quasi-official *démenti* but in fact Canon O'Connell stuck to his point, though the less perceptive thought he had given way'.[11]

What is interesting about O'Connell was that he started life as a rubricist and ended up as a scholarly and pastoral liturgist. Rubricists are generally regarded as a race who wish to maintain the *status quo ante*, but it was interesting to see how, especially in the pages of *Clergy Review*, where he must have instructed generations of priests, he moved with the Church, sometimes to the dismay of the conservatives who felt that the fortress was being mined from within. But what he was doing was no more (and it was a great deal in those days) than to discern what the Church was really saying and to put it before the people with clarity and great common sense.

Nor was his influence confined to the written word. By 1960 his reputation stood very high and he was made a member of the preconciliar commission on liturgy—the only English representative for all that he was a native-born Irishman working in Wales (Menevia). After the Council he was immediately appointed to the *Consilium*, the commission set up to implement the Constitution on the Liturgy. Naturally, he was a member of the English National Liturgical Commission and became involved in the problems of translation. And how should he not be? he who (at first) tackled what came to be known as the Finberg-O'Connell-Knox missal and who liked to say that, as an Irishman, he had a peculiar concern for the purity of the English language! This of course is to anticipate, but the foundations of his contribution to the pre-conciliar Commission, and to the developing liturgy of the post-conciliar years, were laid in the years before the Council.[12]

Rome acts

The first move to come from Rome was the issue of the encyclical letter of Pius XII in 1947, *Mediator Dei*, on Christian worship. Although there was a good deal of 'on the one hand but on the other' in it, to those of good will it was a clear recommendation to study the liturgy, to care for its celebration and to bring about various forms of active participation in it. Promoters of the liturgical movement were of course delighted, but soon enough they had to confront the mini-mizers who said that, while the pope had recommended certain things, like the Dialogue Mass, he did not *order* them, and until he did they would have nothing to do with them. However, one practical result in England was the setting up of the Priests' Association of the Society of St Gregory which owed its origin to Dom McElligott, and was presided over by Francis Grimshaw, then Bishop of Plymouth, one of the very few bishops who knew anything about liturgy or had any care for it. It met for a few years and then died the death. At any time it touched a very small number of priests, though it did much to encourage those who attended its meetings.

It was, however, the formal acts of the Holy See that brought about certain changes that were inescapable. The first, in 1951, was the revi-sion of the liturgy of Easter Eve, which was once again to be celebrated at night. In 1953 there was the permission for Masses in the evening, long desired and needed, with its consequence of the mitigation of the eucharistic fast, first to three hours and then to one. The revision of the Easter Eve liturgy was but the beginning of a revision of the whole of the liturgy of Holy Week which was promulgated in 1955 and came into use the following year. In both these rites English was permitted for the first time as a liturgical language for the profession of faith and the renewal of the baptismal promises. From 1947 until a year or so before the Council new, largely vernacular, rituals were issued for various countries: Austria and France, Germany, Ireland, the United States, and finally England—which had less of the vernacular than any other!

Then in 1958 came the Instructions *Sacred Music and Liturgy*, a title which hardly described its content. Recognizing that for some years there had been a variety of ways in which the liturgy of the Mass was celebrated, and that there were different modes of participation, Rome, as is its wont, wished to put some order into the matter. While there is much about music in the document, its chief importance is that it urged active participation of the people in the Mass. What is more, it suggested ways and means by which this might be done and accepted what had long been a practice in different parts of the Church, that the language of the people could have its rightful places in certain kinds of celebration. Among other things it approved the practice of using a lay-reader for the reading of the liturgy and showed how vernacular hymns could suitably be used *even* at Mass. From a practical point of view it was the most important of all the documents to come from Rome since 1947, and it was indeed the last act of Pius XII before he died. This, if anything, gave both clergy and people all the permissions and encouragement they needed, though it is difficult to gauge its effect in England. If we are to judge by the anguished cries of some in 1964, it might never have been issued.

It needs to be emphasised that both *Mediator Dei* and the Instruction of 1958 were the summing up by Rome and the reinforcement of what had long been taught and practised in various parts of the Church. In the former, the Roman authorities did indeed seem to want to give a *mise-au-point* to the mystery-presence theology of Dom Casel of Maria-Laach, but with certain precautions they endorsed the practices of the wider Church. Likewise the Instruction put in order and encouraged those practices which had now proved themselves as beneficial to the people and really said nothing new. It was the *Church*, in hundreds of dioceses and thousands of parishes, that was on the move; and Rome recognized and endorsed what was happening. Liturgical reform was not produced out of the papal hat, and when the Council met in 1962 it was able to base its findings on what was known (scholarship) and on what was already largely in use. As Pius XII said to the international congress on liturgy that met at Assisi in 1956, the liturgical movement was a sign of the movement of the Holy Spirit in the church.

One last document appeared before the Council. This was the *Rubricarum instructum*, promulgated by Pope John XXIII in 1960. It completed another document, the *Simplification of the Rubrics* (1955), and carried it much further. Neither might seem to be of epoch-making importance, but the former, which was a drastic revision of a mass of disparate and by now disordered rubrics, indicated which way the wind was blowing. It made clear that the liturgical books would have to be considerably revised. Liturgical reform had appeared on the order of the day. It remained to be seen how far it would go.

Towards the Council

Yet when Pope John first 'mentioned' his intention of calling a general council it was not at all clear what sort of assembly it would be. Wittingly or unwittingly, certain Roman authorities gave the impression that it would be a cut-and-dried affair, the endorsement by the assembled bishops of certain documents presented to them by the pope, i.e. the Curia. It would all be over by Christmas. It was not until the end of the first session (1962) that it was possible to discern, through the blanket of non-communication, that the bishops had taken the initiative, that something important was happening, and that among other things the draft of the liturgical constition was a serious and far-reaching document.[13]

Looking over those years from the end of the war to the Council, one has the impression that a great deal was done to prepare the Catholics of England for a reform of the liturgy. Yet it is clear that those efforts were insufficient. There were too few to do too much. England entered the post-conciliar period largely unprepared.

Notes

1   From unpublished material by Fr Clifford Howell.

2   That is to say, it took place in the presbytery alongside, where the chaplain was the exuberant Dom (later Abbot) Philip Langdon, who, for all that he had lived many years in Rome and was familiar with Roman affairs, was in favour of the use of English in worship. Between discussions, he regaled the meeting with inimitably funny stories in Italian and English.

3   A similar society was founded in the USA a little later.

4   The membership of the Society was somewhere between 800 and 1000. Far greater numbers were known to be readers of the Society's journal (as is still the case today) through college libraries, etc.

5   The title remained with his successors until the time when the 'Vice-president' became chairman of the Committee. The Cardinal-Archbishop of Westminster, with two other bishops, has now become the Patron.

6   As recorded elsewhere, shortly before the amalgamation with the Church Music Association, it had once more become *Music and Liturgy*.

7   Concerned in its compilation were Canon A.S.E. Burrett, Fr Clifford Howell SJ, Fr P.W. Stonier (who wrote three hymns for it) and Fr J.D. Crichton.

8   For a further account, see p. 000.

9   Geoffrey Chapman Publishers.

10   Information from Fr Clifford Howell. There were eighteen dioceses at the time.

11   See the present writer's 'Canon J.B. O'Connell' in *Clergy Review*, June 1970, p. 475.

12   A bibliography of Canon O'Connell's books and contributions to the *Clergy Review* will be found after the article cited in the preceding footnote. They consist of 49 items, 16 books and 49 replies. A fuller account by the late Professor Finberg of O'Connell's part in the missal will be found in *Clergy Review*, August 1970.

13   A French translation of the first chapter (draft) of the Constitution appeared shortly after the end of the first session in *Documentation Catholique*.

5 The Liturgical Movement since the Council

H.E. *Winstone*

It is no easy task to write a history of the fifteen or so years since the end of the Second Vatican Council. That there have been considerable reforms in the liturgical life of the Churches—and I am thinking not only of the Roman Catholic Church, but of every other Christian communion with the exception of Eastern Orthodoxy—is obvious to every churchgoer; but these reforms have not yet reached their fruition and we are living too close to the events and have been too involved in them to be able to have anything like a true and unbiased historical perspective.

The immense task presented to the Roman Consilium for the Implementation of the Liturgical Decrees of Vatican II—later (1970) the Sacred Congregation for Divine Worship—to revise the whole corpus of liturgical rites in the light of the new and developing theological, biblical and pastoral insights of the Church is only now reaching its completion. Scholars, experts, pastors, educationalists, men and women with competence in various fields and from nearly every part of the world have been pressed into service. It has been a tremendous achievement and perhaps some of these people are now sitting back to contemplate a job well done. But, in fact, this work is only half done. There still remains the even more difficult task of interpreting correctly the spirit of these reforms and adapting the rites to the needs of the various local communities so that they really do express the life of the community and its self-understanding.

The beginnings of change

The first task of the Bishops of England and Wales was to see that the new liturgical changes were introduced gradually and systematically. As early as 20 October 1964 they published a leaflet 'to the clergy, secular and religious', introducing the 'long-awaited' *Instructio ad Exsecutionem Constitutions de Sacra Liturgia recte ordinandam* and giving guidance in regard to the celebration of Low, High, and Sung Mass, specifying what parts might be said or sung in England.

On 10 March 1965 they issued a further leaflet on 'The Reform of the Sacred Liturgy, second stage: to begin Palm Sunday, 11 April 1965'. In this leaflet they further extended the use of the vernacular at Mass to include all that was said aloud at a Mass with a congregation from the beginning up to the 'Secret' prayer (with the sole exception of the *Kyrie*), and all that was said aloud from the introduction to the Lord's Prayer to the end of Mass, with the exception of the *Domine, non sum dignus,* the *Ite, missa est,* and the blessing. They had already sanctioned a translation of the Ordinary of the Mass (worked out in conjunction with the Scottish hierarchy) which was now made obligatory until such time as it should be revised. Further concessions were made regarding the celebration of Holy Week in English. It is interesting to note the insistence of the bishops on the use of the vernacular. They wrote: 'If a priest wishes to say the Holy Week liturgy in whole or in part in Latin for a good reason (e.g. small texts and failing sight) he may apply to the bishop. It should, however, be borne in mind that the new *Ordo Missae* sanctions the extensive use of lectors.' For parts other than the Ordinary of the Mass, permission was given to use the English translations given in any of the then-current popular missals.

From 1969 onwards the new rites began to come from Rome thick and fast. On the First Sunday of Advent 1969 the revised Order of Mass replaced the old *Ordo Missae* and became obligatory in England and Wales as from 15 February 1970. With it came the new Lectionary. Easter Sunday 1969 saw the introduction of the new rites of Ordination in an interim translation. The new Calendar came into force on 1 January 1970. Easter Sunday 1970 saw the introduction of the new rite for Infant Baptism. An interim breviary was published in Rome early in 1969, and the Irish hierarchy commissioned a translation which became available in July 1970, published by Geoffrey Chapman under the title of *The Prayer of the Church.* The hierarchies of England and Wales and Canada obtained permission from Rome to allow the use of this interim breviary by all who so wished. The Latin text of the Rite of Religious Profession was published in February 1970.

As each of these rites became available, so plans were made for their translation and for their use in England and Wales at the earliest possible date. Not all the changes brought about by the new *Ordo Missae* were introduced at once. The General Instruction on the Roman Missal was a revolutionary document. It shifted the whole emphasis from the rubrical to the pastoral and needed a considerable time to assimilate and for the weighing-up of all the possibilities offered for a genuine celebration of the liturgy in parishes. The greeting of peace was a case in point. A certain reluctance to introduce this was generally evident. In October 1969 the hierarchy decided that experiments might be made in small groups and a report on these sent to diocesan liturgy commissions. It was not until their Low Week meeting in 1971 that they gave general permission for it in any parish that might wish to have it.

The question of translation

The first part of the process of adaptation so far as England was concerned was, of course, the translation of the rites into English. This again was a tremendous undertaking, and all kinds of decisions had to be made before the work could actually begin. Rome had expressed the wish that the same English text should be used all over the English-speaking world, but in England we had our own tradition of liturgical English dating back to the time of the Reformers and even earlier. We could also be said to have a Catholic tradition of liturgical English, the language of the various prayer books and missal translations, culminating in the publication of the *Layman's Missal* shortly before the Council. But this was not a language which some English-speaking countries found acceptable in their worship. They had already, for example, abandoned the thou-form of address—and all the archaic grammatical forms that went with it—in favour of the more direct and prosaic you-form. They had problems with relative clauses in apposition to the deity (*Deus, qui...*) and could in no way come to terms with sacral, or, as they would call them, pious or even 'imperialistic' adjectives.

Immediately after the Council, Archbishop Grimshaw set up the National Liturgical Commission, which immediately set to work translating the Roman Missal as it then was. It began its work by bringing out a translation of the Holy Week liturgy and then turned its mind to the Sunday Masses. At the same time, Rome had brought out a revised text of the funeral rite and released it to the Catholic world in general for comment and criticism. This too was immediately translated and published for experimental use in the parishes. But no one, not even the members of the Committee, was very happy with these results and, after long discussions and heart-searchings, it was eventually decided to scrap this work and to put our resources at the disposal of the International Committee on English in the Liturgy (ICEL).

So ended English efforts at translation, but not altogether England's attempt to be independent of ICEL. We still have our own independent translation of the lectionary responses the funeral rite, the prefaces, prayers and blessings of the Missal, and the *Liturgy of the Hours*. This last is the work of the so-called 'Glenstal-Headingley Committee'. It was commissioned by Bishop Gordon Wheeler of Leeds, then the chairman of the National Liturgical Commission for England and Wales, in consort with the hierarchies of Ireland and Australia and is the only text of this book authorized for liturgical use in these countries. It has proved on the whole to be a very good and successful translation.

Other texts, too, were translated independently—for example, the rite of Confirmation and the Ordination rite—but these were later discarded in favour of the ICEL text once agreement had been reached with ICEL on the translation of the essential sacramental forms. Even though the National Liturgical Commission produced its own version of the prefaces, prayers and blessing of the Roman Missal, the ICEL version was not in fact rejected. The two versions were permitted to co-exist for an initial three-year period so that their relative merits could be tested by actual use. On balance it seems that the ICEL version will eventually carry the day, but neither version is entirely satisfactory. This is not surprising when one considers the immensity of the task and the very considerable difficulties involved in forging a contem-porary liturgical language. In any event, ICEL is committed to review-ing its translations every ten years.

The whole question of the language used in liturgy is an important one and must not be undervalued. The word, after all, is the vehicle of God's revelation of himself to his people. It is likewise the response of his people to his saving presence in their midst. Without the word there is no adequate communication among human beings or between them and God. At the same time, words are quite inadequate to express the mystery of God. He is hidden by the word as well as being revealed in it. Words are likewise inadequate to express the totality of the religious experience of God. It may be that we need a sacral language such as Christine Mohrmann urged in her book *Liturgical Latin*[1] written four years before the Council. A heart that is filled with the realisation of God's overwhelming, saving presence can never find words adequate to express its joyful praise and thanksgiving. There is need for the gift of tongues. But liturgy has to do the best it can for the praise of God and the edification of all who take part in it. As St Paul said: 'In church worship I would rather speak five words that can be understood, in order to teach others, than speak thousands of words in strange tongues.'[2]

There are many perhaps who find the language of ICEL not very conducive to prayer, and they hanker after a more poetic and inspirational language in worship. This may indeed come in time; meanwhile it is fair to admit that, in spite of many false starts and much duplication of efforts, something solid has been achieved, and a member of ICEL might be forgiven for regarding as landmarks in the history of English liturgical renewal the various stages which brought about this achievement. He may remember a winter evening in Rome during the third session of the Council when a group of English-speaking bishops, including Archbishop Grimshaw and Bishop Ellis, sat together in a crowded restaurant and first conceived the idea of setting up a 'liturgical common market'—or that room in the Holiday Inn in Washington where, after months of labour and consultation, a small group of the Advisory Committee of ICEL put the finishing touches to the translation of the Roman Canon and braced itself to meet the storm of criticism and outrage which did not fail to break.

Liturgical Books

A publisher will think of different landmarks. The changes in the rite made the Altar Missal, the *Layman's Missal* and every other missal obsolete overnight; and there was an immediate need for printed texts to put into the hands of priest and people. Without the enterprise and collaboration of our Catholic publishers the changeover would have well-nigh impossible. It was this necessity which mothered the invention of the missalette. One publisher, Burns and Oates, produced a colossal progeny called *Celebrating the Presence of the Lord,*[3] born prematurely and strangled almost before it saw the light of day. Its mother never recovered from the labour and expense of bringing it to birth. Other publishers were more circumspect. They employed expert midwives and filled nearly every Catholic church in the land with their issue.

Yet other publishers concentrated more on the production of liturgical books, and in this respect the record of Geoffrey Chapman is second to none. At a time when the Mass-texts were subject to constant change, they produced two handsome loose-leaf binders with appropriate inserts which could be removed when obsolete and replaced by the newly-authorized texts. One of these binders was entitled *Book of Collects* and was intended for use at the presidential chair. The other was entitled *Sacramentary,* for use at the altar. This showed a fine sense of the requirements of the new liturgy and it is a pity that the principle was abandoned when the definitive text of the Missal came to be printed. For the lectern they produced two versions of the Lectionary, the Revised Standard Version and the Jerusalem Bible.

Their other liturgical books (for baptism, funerals, etc) were of similar quality, and they were the first to publish music for the responsorial psalms by bringing out an excellent—though too little used—edition of the *Simple Gradual*. At the same time they, together with several other publishers, brought out excellent Mass-books for the people; eventually, under the Collins imprint, a comprehensive *Sunday Missal* appeared, every bit as well produced as the preconciliar popular missals.

Education in the liturgy

Education in the new liturgy, and especially in the new pastoral approach to liturgy, was a priority during these years—and indeed still is. What had changed was not just the liturgical texts and ceremonies, but the whole concept of liturgy as something which was no longer the exclusive concern of the priest but of the whole worshipping community. The priest is still the celebrant but, in fact, it is the whole community that celebrates, priest and people together.

Before each of the new rites was introduced into the parishes the bishops insisted on 'adequate catechesis', and it was assumed that the clergy were in a position to give this catechesis. But were they? Trained for many years in the old ways and protected against suspect continental influences, how could they be expected to absorb overnight the new theological and pastoral insights which had influenced the fathers of Vatican II? We had no liturgical institute in this country and very few priests had been sent for training in any of the institutes abroad. Had it not been for the pioneer work done by the Society of St Gregory over many years, the splendid work of such institutes as the Ladies of the Grail, and the dedication of many largely self-taught priests and lay people, the present situation would have been far worse than it actually is. Even so, the situation in many parishes is reflected by the view of a certain parish priest who said to his parishioners: 'I don't like these changes any more than you do, but the Pope says that in future we have to do it this way, and it is our duty as Catholics to do what the Pope says.' So externally the rites have changed, but we are still a long way from absorbing the spirit of the new liturgy.

However, some help was forthcoming. The best of the continental works on liturgy were translated into English and this formed the basis of a post-conciliar liturgical literature which has swelled to impressive proportions. For we were not lacking our own indigenous authors, particularly Fr J. D. Crichton who wrote on the Liturgical Constitution shortly after its appearance and has since put into the hands of English

Catholics several other commentaries together with such excellent treatises as his three books on *Celebration* and *The Ministry of Reconciliation.*[4]

Symposiums such as *The New Liturgy,*[5] *Pastoral Liturgy,*[6] and the most recent ecumenical one, *The Study of Liturgy,*[7] are having some effect, though sales of the first two have not been notoriously high.

At a more popular level we have the various liturgical magazines. That of the Society of St Gregory (*Music and Liturgy,* later *Liturgy,* later *Life and Worship,* later, and once again—after amalgamation with the Church Music Association's journal *Church Music—Music and Liturgy*) has proved itself over five decades. The publishing house of Mayhew-McCrimmon entered the field in 1972 and produced an excellent 'glossy' entitled *Christian Celebration,* which has since amalgamated with the catechetical journal *The Sower* to form *The New Sower.* The Southwark Liturgy Commission did pioneer work in producing *Liturgy Bulletin.* First published in October 1971, this has been the forerunner of several diocesan liturgy magazines. Most recently the National Liturgy Commission, since the establishment of its secretariat in London, has produced *Liturgy* taking over from the Society of St Gregory and the St Thomas More Centre the publication of the former semi-official *Liturgy Newsletter.*

Diocesan commissions

This brings us to the work of the diocesan commissions. Without these the National Liturgical Commission, meeting as it did only once or twice a year, would have been ineffectual in its task of monitoring liturgical education and good liturgical celebration throughout England and Wales. Not all the commissions were equally effective because, as has been seen, there was a great lack of trained liturgists both clerical and lay, but they did provide day and evening courses in the parishes, schools and pastoral centres, and in-service training programmes for the clergy, and they were able to draw upon the expertise of many members of the Society of St Gregory and the religious orders. In 1969 the Westminster Liturgy Commission set up the St Thomas More Centre for Pastoral Liturgy which has not been without its effect nationwide.

At the same time the catechetical centres were having a very great influence on the kind of liturgy that was being celebrated in our schools, and it is perhaps in this field that the greatest advances have been made. The publication in 1975 of the Roman Directory on the Celebration of the Liturgy with Children[8] and the authorization of three new children's Eucharistic Prayers gave a great impetus to this work and released school chaplains from the fear that what they were being urged to do was in some way prohibited. There are problems now in those places where parish liturgies have not kept pace with school liturgies. Obviously, the remedy is not to make school liturgies *less* relevant, but to make the parish liturgy *more* relevant to the needs and concerns of the whole worshipping community. What is happening in schools is a challenge to the parish.

Nor must we forget the quiet yet effective work that is being done in the centres for the handicapped—especially the blind, the deaf and the dumb—and the great efforts that are being made by various agencies to provide appropriate liturgies for the sick and elderly and the housebound. All the time there is this great revolution going on in schools, hospitals, young people's associations, university chaplaincies and seminaries, the combined effect of which is incalculable.

Pastoral liturgy and music

Although the music of this period has been dealt with elsewhere in this book,[9] since it plays so important a part in pastoral liturgy, a few remarks on the matter may not be out of place here. One effect of the changeover from Latin to English was to expose the lamentable state of liturgical singing in many of the Catholic parish churches in this country. The rich Anglican and Free Church tradition of hymnody was no part of our heritage and, in fact, our hymnals excluded any hymns that could not be shown to have a Catholic authorship. Even so, the new Westminster Hymnal of 1939 did admit one or two translations by Anglicans (e.g. J. M. Neale) and the authors of one or two others had a somewhat tenuous connection with the Catholic church.

But what was not generally realised was that the change meant adaptation. By 1970 it was apparent that the form or shape of the Mass had changed. The distinction between 'Low Mass' and 'High (or sung) Mass' was no longer relevant. There could now be singing at all Masses and the question that arose was *what* were we to sing. The new *Ordo Missae* allowed that 'other chants', which for the most part meant hymns, could be used for the entrance and the communion processions and the old *offertorium* was done away with altogether, thus allowing of song of a different sort at the presentation of the gifts. The first difficulty that faced the Catholic community was that we had few, very few, hymns that could be appropriately used at Mass and the need for such hymns led to the making of new hymnals, the editors of which were able to 'spoil the Egyptians'. It was thus that much of the English tradition of hymnody came into common use among us.

But adaptation, one written into the *Ordo* itself, had to go further. There was a new element, the responsorial psalm that is meant, like all psalms, to be sung; and it seemed at first (and there seem to be some who think so still) that we were without musical settings for it. But resources were not so meagre as at first it might have seemed. Père Gelineau had been at work for some years and the English version of his psalter was already available. His work was rapidly followed by that of native composers, particularly Anthony Milner, Laurence Bévenot and Gregory Murray, who put their minds and their talents to the task of setting psalms, as well as antiphons and responsories, to music. The St Thomas More Centre for Pastoral Liturgy in London has encouraged and commissioned a number of young musicians and composers to do the same thing.

Another new element of the rite is that the emphasis on what should be sung has changed somewhat. The General Instruction puts what it calls the ministerial chants (those sung by the celebrant and (often) replied to by the congregation) in the first order of priority. With these must be grouped acclamations, *Alleluia*.... These last are thoroughly congregational chants and deserve great attention. It is true that the community has been well served by young and dedicated composers for the common chants of the Mass, the *Gloria*, the *Sanctus*, the *Agnus Dei*, but it is only in more recent years that composers have begun to realise the musical potential of the ministerial chants and the acclamations. In short, it is now seen by the best composers that when you have written settings for the common texts, you have only *begun* to provide a musical setting for the Mass.

Of the folk idiom in church music it may be said here that from a pastoral point of view it has had its importance in involving the young actively in both singing and making music for the liturgy and thus has done something to prevent a certain alienation of young people from a liturgy (and a Church) that lacks vitality. That was and perhaps still is a real danger. In addition, it has led to the composition of new religious songs reflecting the tensions and challenges of the life of a Christian in the world today. Though some of the earlier songs and melodies appeared to many people banal in the extreme, a refining process is evidently at work which bodes well for the future.

But it is one thing to provide music, quite a different thing to get parishes to sing it. Psalms are obviously meant to be sung but many parishes still fail to sing them. There is still a great lack of trained parish musicians and the standard of singing remains low. Nor is this just a musical matter. Music can bring joy to worship as perhaps nothing else can, and singing can bind together a congregation and give them a sense of community that otherwise they may well lack.

One reason for the continuing low standards is that the strenuous work of the Church Music Association—the executive arm, for a time, of the Church Music Commission—was brought to an end. The tireless efforts of John Michael East, who had stumped the country for months and was producing encouraging results, were deprived of their full effect just at the time when the situation looked hopeful. However, the Church Music Association continues its work as a private society, now happily re-united with the Society of St Gregory; and its members are still active in the liturgical apostolate. Its Composers Group and Organ Advisory Group render very valuable service to parishes who are looking for good music and good instruments. It has close associations with Universa Laus abroad, as the recent Summer School at Strawberry Hill, Twickenham (August, 1978), demonstrated.[10]

Other rites

To give a more complete picture of the post-conciliar situation it would be necessary to consider at some length the impact of the reformed rites for the sacraments. This can hardly be done here; but certain rites, for infant baptism, for marriage and for the care and anointing of the sick all seem to have met with a wide acceptance, at least where they are adequately celebrated. The funeral rite has transformed people's notions of Christian death and is a conspicuous example of the pastoral dimension of the new liturgy. All these sacramental events and others involve priest and people in a common celebration, they all require preparation with the people, and at all of them the word of God is proclaimed. If one wished to assess even now the effect of liturgical reform, it is these matters that should be considered; and if those who write to the press in constant criticism of what has been done to the liturgy of the Mass would do so, they might come to different conclusions.

In yet another area of liturgical practice there are signs of development. Although the structure and details of the Divine Office (*Liturgia Horarum*, 1971; E.T. *Divine Office*, 1974) seemed at first somewhat complicated and not altogether apt for the people's worship, it is proving to be a valuable instrument of prayer. Here and there throughout the country small groups are meeting, whether in church or elsewhere, to recite and sometimes sing the Morning and Evening Prayer of the Church. This was facilitated by the publication of *Morning and Evening Prayer* (Collins, 1976) which many of the laity have taken to with enthusiasm. The same is true of a great number of the clergy and of religious, both men and women, who are not tied to a monastic breviary—though in monasteries, too, there has been a considerable development. Means for an adequate celebration in song of the Divine Office are now being provided. There is the Philip Duffy-Laurence Bévenot group at the Metropolitan Cathedral at Liverpool, there are the psalm-settings of the monks of Mount St Bernard's, there is the Monastic Musicians and Choirmasters Group who meet regularly, and above all, there is *Music for Evening Prayer* (Collins, 1978) which provides settings for Sundays, Holidays and Feasts of the Lord. The whole of this elaborate but very singable project has been compiled by the Benedictine Nuns of Stanbrook Abbey, edited by Hildelith Cumming OSB. With this goes *A Song in Season,* a collection of office hymns. There is here, then, provision for the singing of Evening Prayer for most of the year; it remains for churches to take it up so that the Prayer of the Church may once again become a normal service of parish life.

Church-building

A revolution in liturgical celebration brought with it the need for a revolution in church architecture. In every age, church architecture has reflected the Church's understanding of itself as a worshipping community. The centuries immediately preceding our own have laid stress on the distinction between clerical and lay—the priesthood and the faithful. In our own parlance, the priest 'said' Mass, the people 'heard' it. The priest 'administered' the sacraments, the people 'received' them. This division was reflected in the architectural design of the building. The priest's place was the sanctuary, a raised area cut off from the rest of the church by rood-screen and chancel-(communion-) rail. The priest was the mediator between the people and God—the 'go-between'. The altar, therefore, representing the divine presence (and so usually incorporating the tabernacle) was set against the east wall of the church. The priest thus stood between people and altar, facing the altar, with the people for whom he was making intercession and offering sacrifice behind him.

The two decades after the second world war saw the building of a great number of churches. Many city churches had been bombed and had to be rebuilt. In addition, the post-war period brought with it a great displacement of population. People were moved out of slum city areas and rehoused in suburban estates or satellite towns, where new churches had to be built. A big influx of immigrants from abroad meant larger congregations in many places and local churches had to be enlarged.

All this happened before Vatican II with the result that most of these churches were built in the style of churches of the last century and have had to be adapted, sometimes not very successfully, for the new liturgy. Scant notice was taken of the new architectural designs that had characterized church building on the continent even before the war. There were, of course, notable exceptions in those places where the parish priest, being liturgically erudite and understanding the direction in which things were going, was allowed by the bishop to have his own way.[11]

Since the Council church architects have been faced with a big challenge. They have had to re-think church building not only in terms of the new liturgical requirements, but also in terms of a new understanding of the parish as an outward-looking community at the service of the wider community in which it exists. This has meant the building of shared churches on those new estates where it obviously makes neither good ecumenical nor good financial sense to build four or five separate denominational churches. It has also meant taking account of the need to incorporate into the general ground-plan areas intended for social gathering and community service. Unless our churches are at the disposal of the wider community and serve the various needs of that community, they run the risk of becoming what so many of them already are: private, protected establishments, opened on Sundays for the worship of a minority section of the community, and securely locked for the rest of the time against the possible incursions of society's vandals. How different from the churches of medieval times which were the centre of the life of the whole village!

In recent years many experiments have been made in this area and they are proving highly successful. It is anticipated that the newly-constituted department for Art and Architecture of the National Liturgical Commission will ensure that future church-building will develop along these lines.

But we have still a long way to go. In many instances the re-designing of old—and not so old—churches has been done on the principle that all that needed re-designing was the sanctuary. The altar had to be brought forward, a lectern and presidential chair incorporated, the tabernacle moved to a side-altar, the altar rails taken away, and hey presto, a liturgical church! Little thought has been given to re-designing the church as a whole so as to create a liturgical space in which people can relate not only to the priest and the altar but also to each other in their common celebration of the liturgical mysteries. Too often, after all the labour and expense of re-designing a church, we are still left with fundamentally the same thing: an auditorium and a stage. All that has happened is that the furniture on the stage has been re-arranged—and the actors have new parts. The relation of the people to the sanctuary remains precisely as it was and their active participation just as difficult.[12]

The Secretariat

Finally, a member of the National Liturgical Commission might be forgiven for regarding as landmarks in our liturgical history the establishment of its full-time secretariat in London and the encouragement it has given to the production of pastorally-orientated editions of the Rite of Penance, the Rites of the Sick, and the Worship of the Eucharist outside Mass. It has also spearheaded the programme of catechesis necessary for the introduction of Communion in the hand and, most recently, the reception of communion under both kinds. It has encouraged the commissioning of lay ministers for the distribution of Holy Communion and advised the bishops on the use of the third rite of Penance with collective absolution. It has also presented to the hierarchy positive plans for the long-overdue establishment of a liturgical institute in this country.

These are all solid achievements, and if the full impact of them has not yet reached some of the dioceses and a majority of the parishes, this cannot be laid at the door of the National Liturgical Commission. Education is a slow process, but I believe there is an old Chinese proverb which says 'The journey of a thousand miles begins with one step'.

Notes

1   *Liturgical Latin, its Origins and Character,* Catholic University of America Press, 1957, and Burns and Oates, London, 1959.

2   1 Cor 14:19.

3   For a further account, see below, pp. 128-9.

4   *Christian Celebration: The Mass,* Geoffrey Chapman, 1971;
    Christian Celebration: The Sacraments, Geoffrey Chapman, 1973;
    Christian Celebration: The Prayer of the Church, Geoffrey Chapman, 1976;
    The Ministry of Reconciliation, Geoffrey Chapman, 1974.

5   Ed. the late Lancelot Sheppard, DLT, 1970.

6   Ed. H.E. Winstone, Collins Liturgical, 1975.

7   Ed. Cheslyn Jones, Geoffrey Wainwright and Edward Yarnold SJ, SPCK, 1978.

8   For commentary and text, see Edward Matthews, *Celebrating Mass with Children*, Collins Liturgical, 1975.

9   Cf. pp. 93ff.

10 See *Music and Liturgy*, Autumn 1978, pp. 136ff.

11 Cf. J.D. Crichton, 'A Dream-Church', *Music and Liturgy*, June 1943. The ideas expressed in this article were revolutionary at the time. However, they were eventually incorporated into the design of the new church he built in Pershore, opened in 1959.

12 See *Music and Liturgy*, Winter 1978, pp. 16ff.

6 English Liturgical Music since the Council

John Ainslie

Time was, when the character of the Roman Catholic liturgy was thought of in terms of Latin and plainsong. They were all of a piece—sacral, untouchable and unchangeable. Then, suddenly, they were touched and changed; bishops who would have almost given their lives for the Latin heritage found themselves required by their own voting at the Second Vatican Council to put the reforms into effect. Priests and people obediently did so.

No such appeal to rubrics or loyalty could provide liturgical music in English overnight. When the first English translation of the Ordinary of the Mass was introduced on the First Sunday of Advent 1964, it was made known that, until suitable music was approved by the National Commission for Catholic Church Music, it was forbidden to sing the liturgical texts in the mother tongue. Sung Mass, therefore, still meant the Latin Mass with the readings and a few odd bits in English.

The caution was no doubt timely: 'The future of Church Music is very much in our hands. If we are vigilant and demanding we may lay the foundations of something great. But if we are not, we shall open the door to an influx of shoddy little ditties....' So wrote John Hoban, then editor of *Church Music,* in February 1965. Soon the Commission, with its brief to censor all settings of the liturgical texts, was looking for its first congregational settings of the English Ordinary of the Mass. The trouble was that composers and Commission alike had little experience of what constituted English liturgical congregational music—the existing hymn-tradition was of little help: had any of them ever composed even a hymn-tune for general use? Nor was the whole point of liturgical reform—let alone renewal—explained to them or to anyone else. The old liturgical, i.e. rubrical, technique was to be replaced by a new one—no more.

The introduction of the new Order of Mass in 1970 inevitably constitutes something of a landmark and suggests the following partition of this chapter:

— the period of uncertainty before 1970;
— the period after the introduction of the new *Ordo Missae* when most people thought we had arrived;

— the new period of uncertainty when we realised that we had not arrived and began to learn how to accept responsibility for creating our own liturgical reforms—as the Liturgy Constitution itself had foreseen (art. 37-41).[1]

1.

The first draft of the English translation of the Ordinary of the Mass was lifted at short notice from the existing CTS *Simple Prayer Book* and was never set to music: composers were asked to wait until a second draft became available and to work on that. From the point of view of the translators, there was some sense in this move: they realised that their first draft would soon shown up imperfections in use and their hands would be free to alter the text in the light of experience without having to pacify musicians whose settings of the first draft would thereby become obsolete. But there were several drawbacks: 1) the musicians were left twiddling their thumbs until the second translation became available and 2) there was no opportunity (nor apparently any experimentation) to discover the *musical* requirements of the texts before these were imposed upon them. Had such experimentation been allowed or consultation between text-writers and musicians been held, they would not have been lumbered with:

Glory be to God on high
and on earth peace to men who are God's friends.

This version was largely derived from the Finberg/Knox missal published by Burns Oates at that time and met with particular opposition from the Scots hierarchy: the era of translation with all its problems had indeed arrived. There was also a problem of communication between the National Liturgical Commission, who provided the texts, and the National Music Commission, who were expected to provide congregational music for them—and the Music Commission and composers alike were justified in their resentment. Not only did it lead to a certain distrust of 'liturgical experts' by musicians: the rationale of congregational singing was not made clear and it appeared that the whole choral tradition and the standards of music associated with it were at risk. On the other side, liturgists had little time or temper for musicians who requested a less dogmatic and more sympathetic approach to the development of a new musical language for the new English liturgy.

The situation might have improved when *Musica Sacram*, the instruction on church music from the Roman Commission on Liturgy, was promulgated in 1967. But the conflicting interests in Rome, arising from the same uncertainties as those experienced in the English Music Commission, ensured that the document was ambiguous enough to be read (or misread) according to one's point of view. Despite the efforts of people like Monsignor Wilfrid Purney to keep everyone more or less happy, a number of eminent Catholic musicians opted out of the challenge to compose music for the new liturgy. It was not an exclusively English phenomenon, but one common to Western Europe and North America, where vitriol often took the place of the traditional British reserve.

One facet of the development of post-conciliar liturgy was written into the principles of the Constitution on the Liturgy but was recognized by few at the time. I refer to the development of liturgical pluralism: different approaches to celebration according to the needs and capabilities of the people who make up the present local congregation. The practical effect of this is most keenly felt in the choice of the style of music. Church musicians have the reputation of being dogmatic and single-minded in their opinions on the criteria for good church music. Nowadays room has been found for a number of different musical repertoires to exist side-by-side in the same parish: Latin, sung English and 'Folk'. But in the 1960s the dogmatism of the church musicians was matched by the dogmatism of the liturgist (still chiefly a rubrician). Despite a measure of good will, confrontation was frequent and sometimes bitter.

This was exemplified by the attitude of some of the more zealous clergy towards their church choirs. They appeared to feel that 'participation' required that the congregation should say or sing everything that was not the priest's part and that the choir had no longer any role to play other than support the congregation in the most rudimentary singing. Understandably, choirs viewed with considerable apprehension the settings of the liturgical texts in English written for congregational use. They saw them—and the whole of the vernacular liturgy—as a threat to their established repertoire and status. Nor was there any sign of any new choral music in English or any place in the revised liturgy in which to sing it. How many choirs were actually sacked or resigned over this issue is not recorded (Farm Street choir was a *cause célèbre*, but there were other reasons there); most came to an arrangement whereby Latin and English were alternated Sunday by Sunday, with the choir being given its head at the Latin Masses and therefore preferring them. It is not in the least surprising that many parish choirs have remained the focus of the more conservative voices in parish liturgical committees. The development of a Solemn English Sunday Sung Mass has been accordingly impeded.

It is curious to recall that the only singing in English permitted before the First Sunday of Advent 1966 was at Low (not Sung) Mass—and this with the proviso that what was sung was *not* the official liturgical texts of the Mass! This was a direct continuation of the custom noted in a previous chapter whereby weekday Masses, especially those with children, were enhanced by the singing of English hymns. Such singing was, in a sense, paraliturgical, since such hymns were sung while the priest at the altar 'got on with it'. The hymns were rarely appropriate to the liturgy, if only because the existing hymnals had not been edited with such a use in mind: only Clifford Howell's *Mass Together,* printed privately in 1959, offered a selection of hymns that were really suitable, but this publication (like Fr Howell himself) was frowned upon by 'authority'—at least until 1963, when the advent of the Liturgy Constitution from the Vatican Council vindicated him and a reprint of his hymn-book was hastily put in hand—a total of the order of 70,000 copies was sold.

The other major pre-conciliar preparation for English vernacular liturgy was the Gelineau/Grail psalms, which first appeared in 1955. Aided by the enthusiasm of the Ladies of the Grail and by a delightful EP record of Somerset children singing strange words (psalms) to strange tunes (French) in a strange accent (Stratton-on-the-Fosse), the psalms achieved a remarkable popularity in schools and a few of the more adventurous choirs.

Mass Together and the Gelineau psalms provided much of the inspiration for the series of pamphlets published by St Martin's Publications for Advent 1964. These eventually developed into the 'Parish Choir Book' series, but they started life as 'The Rite of Low Mass arranged with hymns and psalms for...' the various liturgical seasons. They were compiled by the Church Music Association in collaboration with the then administrator of Westminster Cathedral, Mgr George Tomlinson. The hymns and psalms were printed together with their melody-lines (a feature new to Catholic cirlces) and an occasional descant or psalm setting by Fernand Laloux, along with the English texts of the Ordinary of the Mass. Although they had the appearance of being no more then missalettes, they encouraged a flexible and intelligent use of the texts and music available and were just what was required at the time. They were an invaluable aid to a mainly bewildered populace as well as a well-balanced education in liturgical practice. Moreover—and this is probably their most lasting effect—they established the singing of hymns in a liturgical context as a framework for congregational singing. For when, at long last, it became possible to sing the liturgical texts (at least the Ordinary of the Mass) as from the First Sunday of Advent 1966, the bishops of England and Wales formally permitted hymns at the Entrance, Offertory and Communion as constituting the required liturgical music for those parts—even though it was also necessary for the priest to say the missal texts for the introit, etc, to satisfy the rubrics. Moreover, the bishops permitted the use of any recognized Catholic collection of hymns for this purpose—one of their more liberal decisions which has been envied by other Christian denominations who are saddled with official hymnals. By November 1966, Father Wilfrid Trotman's *Praise the Lord* was published, the first English hymnbook specifically for use at Mass, containing a selection of Gelineau/Grail psalms. The *Parish Hymn Book* followed in 1968, a more conservative collection (no psalms) re-introducing relics of a previous age requested (so the Preface says) by the clergy and carrying an air of reassurance, as if to say 'don't worry, nothing has really changed'.

Since then, sales of hymnals have been enormous—despite the use of the parish duplicator, regardless of copyright, and the printing of hymns on Goodliffe Neale's missalettes. Folk hymnals are an extension of the same formula. In many churches, this repertoire of hymns and songs constitutes the corpus of English liturgical music (in some, no other music is heard at all)—in all, they are the most commonly used (and misused) congregational expedient. There is no denying their practicality: even without a keyboard accompaniment, there must be few priests who could not start off 'All people that on earth do dwell' or 'The Lord's my Shepherd'—two examples of the repertoire imported overnight from the newly-acknowledged sister-traditions, whose melodies were already subconsciously known note-perfect through radio and television programmes on Sunday evening—even if Catholic people never admitted to listening to a non-Catholic service....

And what of psalms? There is no denying that the Grail version of the psalms was launched by the Gelineau settings. But whereas the Grail text has established itself unrivalled as the exclusive version in use in England and Wales for the Divine Office as well as for the Lectionary, the Gelineau settings have faded into occasional use alongside the few other available. Why? Because, compared with hymns, they were too much trouble to prepare and sing well. Admittedly, the Gelineau melodies flow less easily in English than in French, due to the different characteristics of the two languages: nor are they practical for large congregations without a great deal of practice. Choirs might well have taken to them, but few saw the point of singing psalms and few found the antiphon-refrains musically satisfying or liturgically significant. As with the hymn itself, there appeared to be too few musicians who could make use of the music in a flexible and imaginative manner. It is a problem that is with us in a more persistent and permanent form—the Responsorial Psalm of the Lectionary, treated so often without music as if it were yet another unintelligible reading.

As for cantors, their introduction in *Musicam Sacram,* the 1967 Instruction, was scarcely taken seriously—there was no one to train them and, in any case, had not Pius X (recently canonized) forbidden soloists in his 1903 Motu Proprio? So when the *Simple Gradual* appeared in 1969, providing officially approved alternative texts for the Proper of the Mass, set to a variety of simpler psalm-tones as well as the Gelineau melodies, it fell upon deaf ears and the cantors and choirs for whom it was designed showed little interest. It had proved the same with the CMA-sponsored *Parish Choir Book* that had preceded it.

In many ways, the choirs could hardly be blamed. Psalms were new and strange to them (some indictment on Catholic education...). Unless they were the privileged few who had taken part in Vespers or Compline (in Latin, of course) and knew what these were about, the most they had seen in their missals were odd verses at the introit, gradual, offertory and communion. Moreover, the tradition of responsorial singing, with an antiphon and psalm-verses sung by choir or cantor, the people repeating the refrain, had never (and has never) become part of English liturgical singing tradition as it has in France and elsewhere.

All might have been rather different if the vital role of the *animateur du chant*—cantor and / or congregational leader—had been realised earlier. The notion that congregations (and choirs too) can simply 'pick up' new music without leadership or direction is both utopian and foolish. The inevitable result was that congregations, told that they ought to sing but not shown how to, picked up only the most repetitive music. Only a little effort in the right place would have enabled them to sing rather better—better music not only in musical distinction but also more uplifting and inspiring music, liturgically speaking. Anthony Milner's Mass (1966) failed to achieve the attention it deserved precisely for this reason.

Milner's was the first of the settings of the Ordinary approved by the National Commission when the second draft of the English translation came into use towards the end of 1966. He had already tried it at a

Summer School in New Orleans in the previous year and had adapted the music to fit the textual variations of the new English version. I do recommend readers who have a copy to look at it again, for it was undoubtedly one of the best settings of that text. The Society of St Gregory Summer School at Manchester in 1969 made a record disc of it, together with the new Order of Mass; unfortunately, production and copyright-administration difficulties gave the record a short life. It is a thousand pities that we have seen so little from Milner's pen to follow the standard he set.

There followed a rush (or rash) of settings of the Ordinary—and most were very ordinary indeed. Except for the special occasion or the rare parish where adequate musical direction was available for the congregation as well as the choir, it was the settings that required no direction and no choir that gained the widest use, in particular, Gregory Murray's *People's Mass* and Wilfrid Trotman's *A People's English Mass*. I do not believe that either composer intended that his setting should be used for ever, yet there are parishes that have been using one or other of these exclusively for the past ten years (Dom Gregory's was amended in 1975 to accomodate the new ICET texts of the Gloria and Sanctus). I do not doubt their value as means of getting the people to sing the Ordinary, but I cannot think that after such 'overtime' there is much freshness in them still to exploit.

For the Proper of the Mass, little was produced at this time, apart from the *Simple Gradual* and an occasional offering in the *Parish Choir Book* series. Meanwhile, the hymn became established as the universal panacea and the three- or four-hymn 'sandwich' became an all-too-familiar programme. There was a perfectly good reason for the unwillingness of composers to tackle the Proper in view of the imminent publication of the new Roman Missal, eventually published in Latin in 1970. When it did appear, the offertory verse had disappeared altogether and the antiphons provided for the introit and communion were not designed for setting to music—even if the English texts had been available. In the almost complete absence of writers of liturgical texts—they had never been *allowed*, now they were *needed*—it is only an unusually imaginative parish that can provide an alternative to the hymn (unless it be Latin plainsong). In view of the psychological importance of the Opening Hymn for setting the atmosphere of the celebration, it is a serious lacuna in the repertoire of liturgical music which even now shows no sign of being filled. The other major lacuna is the Communion Song. Perhaps it is just as well that the rubrics of the Order of Mass prescribe a psalm after the first reading: at least this forces us to take cognizance of texts other than the *Kyrie*, *Gloria* etc., and the overworked hymn. But how rarely it is sung, even in Masses with singing.

Unfairly neglected now is the music that the National Music Commission provided for the minister's chants: the prefaces then in use (twenty or so) with their preparatory dialogue, together with the Lord's Prayer, set to a simplified version of the Latin plainsong formulae. If no masterpieces, the settings were dignified and practical—and infinitely preferable to the ICEL versions which eventually displaced them. It is well to acknowledge Dom Gregory Murray's hand in their composition. Unfortunately, Geoffrey Chapman were the only publishers to print the preface-settings—and only in their loose-leaf altar missal, which was a good liturgical idea but impracticable for bewildered parish clergy: sales were small and usage of the sung preface was thus restricted. The Lord's Prayer was issued on a card by St Martin's Publications, but here the disadvantage was that it was one more piece of paper along with many others that the man in the pew was expected to handle. Yet this was one of the few wholly satisfactory 'plainsong adaptations' to appear with English words; where it was used, it proved to be both effective and memorable.

The National Music Commission, however, was less effective (or memorable) in its role of censor—or, if it had intended to vet every piece of music written for the liturgy, it soon came to recognise that the task was beyond its resources. The approval required for settings of liturgical texts rapidly became a dead letter and in 1969 the Commission itself was dissolved with scarcely a whimper. Its powers and functions were taken over by an enlarged National Liturgical Commission. In theory, the unification should have been beneficial, overcoming the lack of communication mentioned earlier. In fact, the Liturgical Commission was far too busy wrestling with the problems of introducing the new rites and their attendant texts to have time for the music that could have brought those rites and texts to life.

Indeed, there would have been no sponsoring body whatever for liturgical music in England and Wales had not the bishops agreed to support the Church Music Association and so permit the appointment of a full-time salaried director in the person of John Michael East. In return for this bounty, the Church Music Association became the long arm of the hierarchy in matters of liturgical music. With an official mandate from the bishops to conduct a campaign to raise standards of liturgical music throughout the country, John East did remarkable work in the years 1969-73, boosting the sagging morale of many choirs and choirmasters and gaining the respect of as many of the parish clergy as showed any interest in his work. In view of the considerable uncertainties at this stage of the liturgical reform, it was no easy task to gain the confidence of mainly conservative musicians, many of whom knew little about liturgical music and less about the liturgy itself, and to present a balanced instruction in the course of a few hours on a Saturday or a weekday evening which would point the way ahead without offending sensibilities. Nor was the running of the Church Music Association offices in London at the same time as conducting a campaign in the more remote areas of England and Wales achieved without fatigue—and a great deal of dedication in the service of the Church. Since his work as director was ended abruptly when there were no more funds forthcoming to provide his salary, it is only fitting to pay belated tribute to his work.

2.

The new Lectionary came into use with the new Order of Mass in English on the First Sunday of Lent 1970. In retrospect, it is remarkable what little effect it had on musicians' habits. The singing of the proper (i.e. hymns) and of the Ordinary of the Mass (Murray, Trotman, or whoever) continued as before. The innovations of the new Order that required singing—the Responsorial Psalm, the memorial acclamations, etc.—were simply said; despite the appearance of musical settings of these later, they have continued to be said (or mumbled), even though they are parts of the liturgy which, by their nature and function, cry out for song. Why is this so? Because there was no willingness to add to existing tradition and little understanding as to why these new additions should be in the liturgy at all, let alone why they should be sung.

Musicians, like priests, had been used to applying liturgical directives literally and without questioning. The liturgical text was the *datum* and there were usually rubrics governing the way it should be rendered in song. Inevitably, then, the new Order was greeted not only with a sigh of relief ('at long last we have reached the end of the changes') but with the question 'What have I *got* to do to put it into effect?' The question is, of course, quite contrary to the expressed principle of the Liturgical Constitution, written into the new Order of Mass, whereby flexibility and adaptability to local needs and resources is an essential ingredient. This presented the musician with a responsibility for the *liturgy itself,* not just the performance of a given rubric.

Moreover, the new Order gave both the priest and the musician a new role—one scarcely perceived even now—a change from the priest-celebrant *for* the people to the priest-celebrant *with* his celebrating people, leading their worship as president of the assembly—and from the choir-director in his gallery singing *for* the silent congregation to the *animateur du chant* of *the people,* leading their worship in song as co-worker, co-responsible with the priest, and with a function as distinctive as his in relation to the whole assembly. This is not an either/or dichotomy, of course—all development (apart from revolution) is a both/and synthesizing process. But in that development the new element, providing the motive force, needs to be fully recognized and acknowledged.

It is true that, by the early 1970s, it was recognised that the development of the liturgy and its music required a properly integrated effort: when the National Liturgical Commission adopted a new Constitution in 1973, it provided a place for a Music Department and a Department for Art and Architecture as well as one for Pastoral Liturgy—though the Music Department has had little to offer the many musicians who rightly look to it for guidance. National Commissions meeting twice a year, however, are not renowned for inspiring action, and plans for a National Liturgical Institute, which have been on the agenda of the meetings of the National Liturgical Commission for ten years, were deferred once again in 1978.[2] The reunification in 1975 of the Church Music Association with its parent, the Society of St Gregory, has assisted what was the policy of both organizations—namely the proper integration of music in the liturgy which it serves and helps to create; both the contents and name of the magazine resulting from the amalgamation, *Music and Liturgy,* bear witness to this.

Dioceses and other regional or local groupings have an enormous advantage over national bodies: they can see themselves and be seen to be concerned with the 'grass-root' needs. As one might expect, dioceses which had either a strong and active Diocesan Liturgical or Music Commission or an established diocesan branch of the CMA (which continued under SSG aegis after amalgamation) have done rather better in raising standards of liturgical music than dioceses that have neither. Commissions that put out questionnaires indicate dioceses that are alive to what is already being done and wish to improve it. The surveys conducted by the Liverpool archdiocese in 1972 and the Portsmouth diocese in 1976 are therefore not typical of other dioceses, but they do show some interesting facts that might well be verified elsewhere. In each case about 60% of the parishes replied to the questionnaire, all of whom had singing at Sunday Mass on a regular basis: 16 parishes in Liverpool (11%) could boast singing at every Sunday Mass. Those who did not reply to the questionnaire might be assumed

to have less interest in church music and at least some of these probably and little or no singing. 70-74% of parishes had adult choirs and
54-59% children's choirs—a surprisingly high proportion; but whereas half (49-51%) of parishes sang the Ordinary of the Mass, nearly half
of these (22-24% of the whole) used Gregory Murray's *People's
Mass*—settings more suitable for choir and congregation are hardly
mentioned. Although 25 parishes in (18%) in Liverpool in 1972 had
Ordinaries sung by the choir alone, it appears that in general choirs
were assuming their role of leading the congregation, but the data
make one wonder how many were making a distinctive contribution *in
partnership* with the congregation. By 1976, however, 32% of Portsmouth parishes were regularly using 'folk' settings of the Ordinary, of
which more anon, and the number of parishes singing the Responsorial Psalm had risen from Liverpool's 14% in 1972 to 37%. The data
for hymns from the two surveys are less comparable—what is disturb-
ing in the Liverpool survey is that nearly half the parishes (47%) used
duplicated sheets for hymns. While it is possible that the more conscientious parish sought out only those hymns in the common
domain, one cannot but wonder at the extent of infringement of
copyright.

Quite how and where 'folk' music came to be an acceptable part of
the new liturgical repertoire is difficult to determine. It had little to do
with Geoffrey Beaumont or the Twentieth Century Church Light
Music Group with which his name is associated,[3] though the music
produced by the members of this rather isolated team may have contributed to a certain loosening-up of attitudes in some quarters (and a
hardening of them in others!).

From the early 1960s onwards, the music of people such as Sydney
Carter and Hubert Richards became increasingly well known in guitar-
ists' circles. Their texts were often scripturally based, or provided un-
comfortable comment on matters of social concern, and were backed
up by music of quality. In schools, many nuns were taking up the guitar under the influence of catechetical experts such as Mother (later
Sister) Mary Oswin; but with few exceptions both texts and music from
such sources have proved to be ephemeral and only recently have compositions of more distinctive textual and musical quality appeared.

A key factor in promoting the best of such music was Corpus Christi
College,[4] England's national catechetical training-centre in Notting
Hill, just next door to the Notting Hill Ecumenical Centre (at that
time the only one in the country). Sydney Carter was frequently to be
seen at the Ecumenical Centre, as was Hubert Richards, the Director of
Corpus Christi. Carter's work had been published, at first informally,

from the late 1950s, and had not yet been caught up by the larger commercial firms; his influence was principally in non-conformist circles.

The first watershed came in 1967 when Geoffrey Chapman published the *Gospel Song Book,* edited by Malcolm Stewart, himself an accomplished guitarist and composer/text-writer and—more importantly—a friend of both Carter and Richards. The *Gospel Song Book* brought together between two covers the best of the work of Carter, Richards, Peter de Rosa, Nigel Collingwood, Mary Oswin and Malcolm Stewart himself, along with some splendid examples of traditional songs and Negro Spirituals from the USA. Although the book did not sell in vast quantities, its influence was enormous—and not only within the Catholic Church. It is interesting to note that it is only by a historical accident that we do not now refer to 'gospel songs' rather than 'folk music': in the middle and late sixties the term was almost universally the former, the latter replacing it at the time when American imports began to flood the repertoire.

The *Gospel Song Book* was followed by other collections from the pen of Richards and others. These maintained the exceptionally high standards of the earliest days, and it would be true to say that little written since has equalled, let alone surpassed, them. But then less sensitive composers and musicians began to write and use material whose taste left something to be desired. As on the Continent, where the folk-music movement got under way at about the same time, we have suffered from the cult of personalities. The principal American influence appears to have arrived with a group of Jesuits (St Louis), a group of Anglican Benedictine monks (Weston Priory) and some Medical Mission Sisters (led by Sister Miriam Therese Winter). Without the aid of records (and later cassettes), their bland productions would never have had the success over here that they in fact received.[5]

By the early 1970s, the style was too prevalent to be ignored and the editors of the revised and enlarged edition of *Praise the Lord* felt obliged to include a small selection of the better compositions. Mayhew-McCrimmon espoused the tradition more fully and expanded it in the *20th Century Folk Hymnal* series (continued by Kevin Mayhew Ltd), later incorporating much of the material in their *Celebration Hymnal.* Some of the most recent publications, now that the movement has been in full swing for a decade, are starting to revert to the Sankey-and-Moody sentimental numbers of the last century, taken over virtually unaltered from the original productions. This does not bode well for the future.

What was the rationale of such music? Many well-intentioned nuns, teachers and later priests thought that such 'folk music' would appeal to teenagers and young people generally and so encourage them to participate in the liturgy instead of walk out from it. The term 'folk music' is, of course, misleading. There is nothing, for example, to link it with the English folk-song tradition, whatever that may be and even though it may be dead. The name was no doubt coined partly because some of the early repertoire was imported from the United States, where it *might* have been called folk music with some justification, partly because it was felt that the style had something in common with the musical tastes of today's younger generation and with their sub-culture. But it has never been persuasively shown that, whatever young people may find attractive to listen to in a disco (and perhaps to participate in by 'dancing'), they will find attractive to sing in church. Further, the style is unsuitable for singing by large congregations without at least as much practice as the singing of a new plainsong Mass (e.g. *Cum jubilo*) in former times—more so if the only accompaniment provide is a guitar rather than the organ, since guitars, even amplified, have insufficient 'bite' to keep a whole congregation singing together and to give them the support they have come to expect from the organ.

Do not misunderstand me. I am not against the use of the guitar or any other musical instrument in church: 'reverence' and 'dignity' are not incompatible with joyful enthusiasm, which the 'folk' idiom has certainly brought to many celebrations (how often do the psalms speak of 'exultation', 'jubilation', etc?). My complaint is that the idiom has been too often put to the wrong use. As the young generation know it, it is meant to be sung by a soloist or small group and it is in this manner of performance that it is at its most effective in church, with rare exceptions. Both the style of music and the scoring of the accompaniment call for this—so do many of the lyrics: for a large congregation to sing 'It's me, it's me, it's me, O Lord, standing in the need of prayer' to a tune crying out for a soloist or small group strikes me as sheer absurdity. Group Masses are another matter.

Indeed, it may be noted that I have said nothing about the words in describing the idiom. 'Liturgical folk' arrived because of the music. Like most second-rate 'folk-pop' (and most second-rate hymns) it is the tune that is memorable—the words are best forgotten. The few really remarkable creations in 'liturgical folk', as in hymnody, have resulted from the fusion of good words with good music—and I can think of few rivals to Sydney Carter in this connection. A vaguely Christian theme does not entitle a text to liturgical use: and this is as valid for the 'folk' repertoire as for hymnals in the more traditional mould and many of the polyphonic motets of yesteryear.

My criticism is not aimed at the conceptual content of the words alone, nor at their expression. I am well aware that I would be unable, if challenged, to provide a satisfactory explanation in a few words of what constitutes *liturgical* music. But I am concerned with the integration of the style of language and music of the 'folk' (and any other idiom) with the liturgical texts of the Mass. The latter have been composed, first in Latin and then in their English version, with a traditional concept of solemn and formal liturgy in mind—and it happens that traditional hymns integrate tolerably well with this (I am less sure that ICEL translations and Latin plainsong make good partners). 'Liturgical folk', however, is of the informal, hail-fellow-well-met style, both in music and lyrics, and it therefore requires an informal style of liturgy to suit. This approach may indeed be putting the cart before the horse—but there are plenty of arguments for developing a more informal style of liturgy in any case.

The hymn is dead: long live the hymn. Indeed, the hymn tradition is long past its best and we badly need fresh texts and fresh music in new styles for choral and congregational singing. Father James Quinn's *New Hymns for All Seasons* offers some useful new scriptural hymns but keeps within the traditional hymn metres. The congregation need not sing everything: we also need material in which the congregation's participation will be less vocal but not less *actual* (rather than active), i.e. by listening and by silence. Such a statement might have seemed anathema to liturgical zealots (perhaps even myself!) ten years ago, but we do need to achieve a new balance in the planning and celebration of the liturgy in which the whole nature (and mystery) of worship is more sensitively and perceptively handled. In this balance, cantor and choir (or vocal group) will have their part to play—and that cantor or vocal group may well find a new prayerfulness for themselves and the congregation with whom they sing and pray 'liturgical folk'.

3.

Sing the Mass, published by Geoffrey Chapman in 1975, was 'a new source-book of liturgical music for cantor, choir and congregation' (so ran the sub-title). Edited by a panel of notable liturgists as well as musicians, chaired by Nicholas Kenyon, it contained contributions by most, if not all, of the qualified musicians composing for the English liturgy in the United Kingdom at that time. It was challenging in two ways: not only did it present the user with the responsibility of

choosing the music that best suited his resources (for it included settings of varying difficulty), but it also made him ask questions about
the liturgy itself. What was the purpose of this or that part, that the
music to which it was set should be treated in this or that way? How
does a sung text integrate with what comes before and after it in the
liturgical rite? What parts should receive sung treatment in preference
to others and why?

Although the excellent introduction to *Sing the Mass* showed the
reader how to ask and answer such questions, church musicians were,
in general, unaware that such questions existed. We have all of us
been too accustomed to thinking of the liturgy as a concatenation of
prescribed 'bits'. Too rarely have we looked at the whole celebration—together with the people who take part in it—and tried to discern its overall structure and *movement*. It may be that the cosmopolitan nature of the congregation will require an approach that will have
more in common with a multi-coloured kaleidoscope being vigorously
shaken than with the characteristic ethos of an entirely uniform Latin
plainsong Mass. But all good liturgy has a shape and form, a rhythm of
its own to which its participants will respond if given breathing space
(moments of silence) and a little sensitive encouragement. It is a living
action, both in what it signifies and in what it demands of the
celebrating participants, in which the high points of *élan* need to be
balanced by times for rest and meditation. As in a symphony, there
will be peaks of exultation contrasting with, and lending effect to,
moments of calm. The liturgical rites, too, provide potent *tempi forti*
of jubilation alternating, within each 'movement' of the liturgy, with
spaces for reflection (cf. the traditional *spatium paenitentiae*). But,
like the printed music of a symphony, the rites themselves will be
lifeless unless, like the conductor of a symphony, the liturgical
musician can discern the high and low points of this celebration with
this congregation and use the music to breathe the spirit of worship in
the hearts of the people. *Sing the Mass* attempted to illustrate the
need for such sensitivity; perhaps it was a prophet before its time, but
it will surely come into its own in years ahead.

As a publishing 'package', *Sing the Mass* arose out of the increasing
difficulty experienced by the larger publishing-houses in the early
1970s in producing and handling sheet music, e.g. settings of the
Ordinary of the Mass. Geoffrey Chapman opted out of this altogether,
but Mayhew-McCrimmon, with its rather more restricted objectives
and scale, has continued to provide settings in a variety of styles. However, the last few years have seen the emergence of the one-man
cottage-industry publisher of liturgical music: Chiswick Music (Bill

Tamblyn), Clifton Music (Christopher Walker), Portsmouth Publications (Geoffrey Boulton Smith), Magnificat Music (Paul Inwood) and Parish Music (Philip Duffy). The important feature common to all these imprints is that they have arisen out of local needs; moreover, the music they publish is itself based on personal experience of the liturgy at local level, created by the needs of those who celebrate it. Here indeed is the right approach and it matters less that they should be successful publishing ventures (which we hope they will be) than that they afford sorely needed encouragement for parish and school musicians to adopt a similar attitude in their own circumstances.

The introduction of any new music requires a little imagination and vision. The greatest enemy of such a vision is PDML—the pre-determined (or pre-digested) mass-leaflet or package-deal missalette. My objection is less to the concept than to the attitude it can so easily produce among priest and people alike. To get the Catholic population used to the rubrical technique of the new Order of Mass when it was introduced, missalettes were undoubtedly helpful. When they are seen as no more than aids to worship, to be used with selectivity and discernment, I have no objection. But they lead too easily to a mindless, slavish adherence to the printed word, the ritual utterance of which is deemed to be liturgy, executed, as one of the contributors to this book once remarked, with all the enthusiasm of filling in one's income-tax return. They have undoubtedly inhibited growth in understanding and appreciation of liturgical *worship* as something not contained *ex opere operato* in the words but to be created in the hearts and minds of the worshipping community.

It would have been out of place to make remarks such as these in this chapter on liturgical music were it not for the deadening effect on the development of liturgical music that the missalette-attitude to liturgy has inculcated. Missalettes that contain hymns are the worst offenders in this respect, since this relieves that choirmaster as well as the priest of any need to prepare the liturgy at all, contrary to all the injunctions of the liturgical documents. Like the use of the traditional hymn itself, it makes it all too easy. It is the death of liturgical music because it is the death of liturgy. Familiarity breeds contempt—unless it is used as a starting-point for growth.

There are hopeful signs of such growth in liturgical music—from the one-man publishers mentioned earlier, in particular. If we are less dogmatically certain, as musicians, of what we are supposed to be doing and how, this may well be a good thing—for it may show that we have realised that our subject is not texts or music but worship; and that we are being called to express, more tentatively but not less confidently, something that is both far away and also within our hearts.

Notes

1   The writer is indebted to Geoffrey Boulton Smith for providing documentary material for this chapter.

2   The urgent need for such a National Liturgical Institute was recognized by the Society of St Gregory as long ago as 1956.

3   The importation of J.M. Brierley's hymn-tune *Camberwell* for 'At the name of Jesus' is a quite recent addition to the folk repertoire. Indeed, it is so 'straight' that it might be more correct to think of it as an addition to the lighter side of the classical hymnody scene.

4   Corpus Christi College was closed down in 1972 by the late Cardinal Heenan, amidst considerable outcry.

5   See also below, p. 117.

7 Influences on the English Liturgical Scene

Kevin Donovan SJ

As I began this chapter, I asked a friend who is interested in liturgy and church music what influences he thought there had been in the last fifteen or so years. He reflected for a moment, then answered: 'Not many, really. After all, nothing very much has happened, has it?' A bit harsh, perhaps, as a summary of the liturgical movement in England, but then this was a priest who had studied for three years at an American university, doing parish supplies throughout that period. But he may be right when it comes to assessing the influences that have actually been at work. And *how* do you assess influences? There have been few surveys on the liturgy in this country, and fewer still have included questions about which influences have proved most important. So there is a shortage of hard data, and one is thrown back on subjective impressions. Indeed, this must inevitably be the case when it comes to ascribing relative weight to different possible influences. What follows, then, is based on one man's assessment of the English scene, derived from personal observation, reading and also discussion with others. It concentrates on England, and does not include Ireland, Scotland and Wales. It concentrates on the liturgy of the Mass, believing that what is true of the Eucharist is, broadly speaking, true of the other sacraments as well. It would certainly take us too far afield to deal with the specific problem of the new rite of Penance and its effect in this country. The influences listed are varied. There are authoritative documents from Rome, official bodies in this country, trends from abroad, the work of individual priests and groups dedicated to liturgical renewal. Finally, and most important—but also the most difficult to pin down—the inspiration and mysterious workings of the Holy Spirit. Dear reader, if you disagree strongly with the following analysis, it would be good to hear your views.

First beginnings

England played virtually no part in developing the early stages of the modern liturgical movement. Scholars there had been, like Edmund

Bishop or Dom Connolly of Downside. They were historians, however, rather than pastoral liturgists. It was left to the mainland of Europe to produce the blend of scholarship and pastoral concern which marks the liturgical movement proper. There is no need to trace again its history since the work of Pius X and the clarion-call of Dom Lambert Beauduin before the first world war. They found echoes in these islands, not only among Catholics but also among Anglicans like A.G. Hebert, with his championing of the Parish Communion and the complementary need for the Church to be involved in social questions. At this stage, however, there was little direct influence between those who were working for Prayer Book reform and Catholics concerned to popularize plainsong and the Dialogue Mass. Here, pride of place must be given to the Society of St Gregory and its continued work, first under the inspiration of its founder, the late Dom Bernard McElligott, and then under his successors. This sustained effort obviously includes all that was achieved by the daughter-organization, the Church Music Association, and the publications which gave the work a wider diffusion and a more permanent form. In the days before the Council, the liturgical movement tended to be a matter of personal conversion. A number of priests were formed by the Society of St Gregory, and several parishes radiated an important influence. Without pretending to be exhaustive, one could mention the inspiration given since the war by those of Cockfosters with its Benedictine community headed by Dom Edmund Jones, Pershore under Fr J.D. Crichton, and Westbury-on-Trym under Mgr Joseph Buckley. These are only outstanding examples. The great peripatetic apostle of these years was obviously Fr Clifford Howell SJ. These were all pioneers, and, like pioneers, were often unfairly criticized. The truth of the matter is that England was unprepared for the impact of Vatican II, particularly on the liturgy. We had suffered during the war. We had even won it. But we had never experienced the disruptive influence of invasion and occupation. Few of our priests, fewer still of our bishops, had seen the inside of a concentration-camp. Yet these are experiences that give a sense of perspective. I shall never forget the story I once heard of a group of priests, newly arrived in Dachau, who lamented that, if only they had had vestments, they could have said Mass....

At all events, we had our few prophets, themselves indebted to the Continent. As is the way with prophets, they were sometimes stoned, and their words disregarded. Symptomatic of the state of the country as a whole was the cool response given to the renewed Easter Vigil. Even now, it scarcely vies in popularity with Midnight Mass at Christmas. Came the Council, and we had to learn new ways. The decisive influence here was of course the Liturgy Constitution itself, and the subsequent publication of revised rites and a new Missal. These were accompanied by commentaries, official and unofficial. Most dioceses decided to have study-days for the clergy. Attendance varied. So did the degree of enthusiasm. But even when there was a three-line episcopal whip, many priests found it difficult to welcome the changes wholeheartedly. As Archbishop Dwyer of Birmingham once pointed out, what was needed was a change of heart, not just a change of rubrics: but the heart was still for the old ways which had been good enough for the English Martyrs or the days of the Potato Famine. Still, the English are an obedient race, as the bus-queues testify, and we obeyed the documents coming from Rome. Liturgical commissions were formed, at national and diocesan level, and these addressed themselves to the patient task of digesting decrees and then regurgitating them in more palatable form. How many priests, one might ask, have actually read the General Instruction to the new Missal? In spite of this reluctance, the influence of Rome has been decisive. What of other factors, from Europe or America?

The European scene

If it is true that the British Isles were unprepared for the liturgical movement, which began in Europe and had hardly reached this country by the time of the Council, how much truth is there in the view that the Continent was ready a long time before ourselves? The beginnings of the liturgical movement are usually dated from 1909, with a prophetic lecture given by Dom Lambert Beauduin on the need for participation by the faithful. Not many people can now remember his urgent call, but one of those who did was a phenomenally learned and craggy monk called Bernard Botte. Sixty years later he was at pains to put on record his personal account of what had happened since the last years of Pius X. Initially, Dom Lambert felt that the best way to reach the people and help them become praying communities was through their priests. His first concern was thus to alter the whole theological and mental attitude of parish clergy, trained as they had been in an era when rubrics reigned supreme. Hence his insistence on the need to study the genuine Roman tradition as it was before clericalism, individualistic piety and peripheral devotions had threatened to distort the vision of the Church and its liturgy. The great abbeys of Belgium, and soon of Germany, devoted themselves to this work. Much of this is familiar enough, although seldom as well told as in *Le mouvement liturgique* (1973). Botte's humour is mordant, as his pupils will remember. What is fresh are the delightfully frank portraits of the protagonists, and the considered judgements about the origins and progress of the movement, including occasional aberrations and not infrequent brushes with the Roman bureaucracy.

Perhaps the most interesting observations concern the very recent emergence of the idea of actually reforming the liturgy. Botte is quite clear about this: at its inception—that is to say, before the First War—there was no question of changing rites or texts (p. 32). The same is true of the inter-war years (p. 74). It was recognized that there was indeed room for improvement, but throughout this period it was a case of making the most of what there was. A good example of this would be the early meetings of the YCW under the then Abbé Cardijn. These were held at Botte's own Abbey of Mont-César, Louvain. The Latin chant was rehearsed by one of the monks; and the crowds of young workers sang it lustily, as well as forming an offertory procession and all going to Communion. Occassions like this had far more effect than a dozen articles. But it was only in German-speaking countries, under the influence of Pius Parsch, that there seems to have been much of a push for the use of vernacular hymns and chants during the liturgy. Between the wars, there was a distinct coolness on the part of the Roman Curia, with somewhat reluctant permission for Dialogue Masses. It was almost as though the reforms initiated by Pius X had been put into cold storage. The rise of Hitler, followed by the war, brought at least the scholarly side of the movement virtually to a standstill. And yet, as chaplains and ex-servicemen will testify, war and imprisonment can bring a new depth to one's appreciation of the liturgy.

At all events, it was in the last years of the war that things began to move in France, a country until then relatively untouched by the liturgical movement. The initiative here was with a semi-private venture, the Centre de Pastorale Liturgique, which did eventually acquire official episcopal backing. In the late 1940s, the work was still twofold—scholarly, and more directly pastoral. A convenient edition of early liturgical and patristic texts, with translation and commentary, was begun. Groups of specialists met by invitation each summer to share the fruits of their researches. But now those who took part included parish priests of long experience, YCW chaplains, others connected with the worker-priest movement, and active religious. This cross-fertilization was made available for a wider audience through summer schools, which were soon attended by several hundreds of participants. One of the best-known products of this period was the setting-to-music of the psalter of the Jerusalem Bible: a whole approach to the use of the psalms in the liturgy will henceforth be associated with the name of Gelineau. In English translation (as the 'Grail Psalter'), this venture has had considerable impact in this country. It was soon followed by the Deiss and other settings of other biblical canticles. These, however, did not find their way across the Channel in any significant quantities until the late 1960s. The 1950s saw the beginnings of international congresses of liturgical scholars, including some who had worked as missionaries. For the first time, the subject of liturgical reform was seriously raised. Among the first questions to be discussed were concelebration, the revision of the Roman Canon, the place of a penitential rite in the Mass. One year, adult baptism was the theme. Would it not be more advisable to drop the exorcisms? Up spoke a missionary—the catechetical expert Fr Hofinger: in his experience, exorcisms were of vital importance. And suddenly, it became clear to many at the congress that they were not working merely for Europe but for a worldwide Church. The liturgical movement had come of age.

To return to our original question: was the mainland of Europe so much better prepared for the Council and its reforms than ourselves? The answer has to be a qualified 'Yes'. Europe is not a single country, and it makes a considerable diference whether you have in mind Europe behind the Iron Curtain, or in the affluent West, a minority Catholicism as in Scandinavia, or a Church buttressed by a concordat: and even in the same linguistic region, town and country are often very different. Having said that, it is clear that Belgium, Austria and Germany had enjoyed fifty years of scholarly discussion, study-weeks and popular writing about the liturgy to draw on. In other countries, notably France, the impetus came only after the war; but lost time was soon made up. This, however, is not to say that before the Council every parish was a model that we could envy. On the contrary, then, as now, it was certain centres that stood out. In Germany there was the work of the Oratorians in big cities like Munich and Frankfurt. This was at parish-level, but there was also a fairly elaborate system of youth-centres with specialist chaplains. In France, the work of the YCW and parallel organizations has been mentioned. In Paris, the university parish of Saint-Séverin became widely known and its *équipe* published many books and pamphlets. A rather earthier approach could be found in working-class suburbs associated with Abbé Michonneau's *Mission de France* and the *Fils de Charité*. And there was the great ecumenical phenomenon of Taizé, with a Catholic-inspired liturgy that was years ahead of the Catholics and had a tremendous influence on young people. Significantly, in all these instances, the clergy concerned worked very much as a team, and made sure that lay-helpers were fully involved. Slowly but surely, the influence of such centres spread within the limits of the old liturgy. Visitors from England and elsewhere came and learned. But the cumulative effect of all this preparatory work was really seen when the Liturgy Constitution, itself largely the work of continental scholars, was finally propagated. Where we, frankly, were left largely floundering, the Continent already had national organizations, several liturgy institutes for training the clergy, and a growing body of experienced priests and musicians.

Since then, progress has not been uniform. The most original developments have probably been in Holland, which has produced the striking texts of Oosterhuis (widely available in English) and the equally magnificent music of Huijbers (less well known, but the product of a man who is arguably the finest liturgical composer now writing—and his theories and writings on the subject of 'The Performing Audience' and 'elementary music' have proved of seminal influence, spread abroad by the agency of international study-groups such as Universa Laus). Searching and profound as is the liturgy in the Dominicuskerk, and the student community, of Amsterdam, it must be admitted that it has not always travelled well, even inside Holland. This has to do with the advanced theological options of the particular groups from which this sort of liturgy has emerged. It would be to a certain extent true to say that the most interesting liturgical developments taking place in Holland today are in the context of a Church that has gone substantially 'underground' to escape what are seen as the petty, unthinking restrictions of the Roman Curia.

In French-speaking countries there has also been a prodigious effort at creating texts and music of varied quality—some very high—as a new tradition of singing was built up. The result of this effort could be seen in the fact that, in the comparatively short space of time between the end of the war and the promulgation of the Liturgy Constitution, the French had carved out for themselves a whole new tradition of vernacular singing at Mass, and were thus not caught napping by the reforms and had a solid foundation on which to progress. It could also be seen in the international stature of some of its leading musicians and textualists. What strikes the visitor is a recognizably French approach to liturgical celebration, due in no small measure to impressive organization, training and the provision of nationally-produced resource-material on a scale unknown over here. Nevertheless, there are dangers in this, too. Quite apart from the tremendous amount of dross appearing (inevitable with anything up to 200 new publications coming out every week), the musical field has been totally reorientated by the record-player: where previously successful performance would be followed by sheet-music publication on a *fiche,* with eventual recorded performance for the best material, now the pattern has reversed itself; everything now appears on disc first of all, and only the material that is easily learnt from the record stands a good chance of appearing as a *fiche.* Although the majority of people consider this trend to be a bad thing, there seems nothing much to be done about it. The same thing may happen in England one day as a result of the large quantities of liturgical folk-music cassettes now starting to mushroom. We have other lessons to learn, too. The French have realised that there is a difference between good poetry and good liturgical texts. A quantity of the official texts (now replaced or optional) were produced with the collaboration of a leading French poet. They proved uniformly disastrous.

Northern Italy and parts of Spain are very much akin to France in their approach to liturgical celebration; though the Italians—now very active—have a tremendous problem with a general lack of good taste (perhaps over-romanticization would be a better description) in both texts and music, still to be overcome; in Spain, most young people seem to have stopped coming to church altogether, leaving the older people attempting to celebrate in a tradition that they have not yet really made their own.

Germany began with the great advantage of its musical and chorale tradition; but is now, according to some accounts, in danger of getting into a rut. The bishops, in agreeing to impose a national service-book, appear to have overlooked the fact that in so doing they are stifling any further musical (or textual) creativity; while many pastors appear now to have reverted to a kind of latter-day rubricism, substituting a new set of regulations for the old ones, and becoming content once again to cease using their imaginations.

All of which goes to show how difficult it really is to attempt to generalize nowadays. One thing is certain—the original debt of the liturgical movement in this country to the work of pastors, liturgical scholars, authors and musicians from Europe.

American influences

What of America? In pre-Laker days, few of us had been there to see for ourselves. But here again, books and music meant that something of transatlantic Catholicism and its experience became available in England. At the official level, there is the work of the ICEL translators.

These cannot be labelled as exclusively American merely because the headquarters are in Washington DC.[1] But in their alternative collects one might detect a marriage between Rome's authorization of a more creative style of translation and the actual experience of writing your own prayers. To do this well requires a sensitive blend of skills, and also the practice which can only be acquired through trial and error. Now, it is a fact that this has happened on a much wider scale in North America than in other parts of the world. There is nothing in Britain like the large American university campus, many of them Catholic or with a sizeable Catholic population. The sort of liturgy that has developed in this milieu seems to me to have had a considerable influence on the texts, music and style of celebration in student chaplaincies and, to a lesser extent, school communities. Although England has never had an 'underground Church', there is no doubt that published collections of American prayer-texts have been used in the Eucharist. More widespread, and less problematic, has been the use of American folk-hymns and others inspired by them. The music, especially to begin with, was often of a simplicity that made professional musicians wince, but it worked. The controversy over the merits of 'instant music' in the liturgy will probably continue—and so will its use. Certainly, the sound of guitars and percussion in the liturgy has had the effect of desacralizing church music. The words of these hymns were sometimes sentimental, or rough paraphrases of the Bible. But at their best they had a social relevance, a commitment to the Gospel values of justice and peace which made a welcome and needed change from the almost unrelieved diet of hymns to Our Lady, the Sacred Heart and the Blessed Sacrament to which English Catholics had subjected themselves. And then there was the much livelier and even uninhibited style of celebration. True, there were aberrations and ill-thought-out excesses of the doughnut and Coke variety. Yet something of all this was wanted in the Old Country. The very success of the English folk-hymn industry is proof enough; and this only obeyed the laws of supply and demand. In every parish in which they were introduced, Folk Masses soon established themselves as probably the best attended and popular Mass of the Sunday, sung Latin notwithstanding. Of course, this trend has not been confined to England but is worldwide. However, if only for linguistic reasons, it is fair to speak of a particularly American influence, helped by a generous supply of recordings made by groups of photogenic monks and nuns. Superficial and short-lived? Some may think so, but only time will tell. At any rate, we may be grateful that some of America's turgid, sentimental and overdressed trends in the 'serious' liturgical music field have not also come to beset us.

As for the second wave of American influence, there can by now surely be no questioning the importance of the movement best known as Charismatic Renewal. This is primarily concerned with prayer and openness to the action of the Holy Spirit, rather than with providing 'creative and meaningful liturgy'. But it does have an important bearing on liturgy itself. It emphasizes prayer and the experience of prayer, especially the prayer of praise. It values spontaneity, encourages improvisation and free prayer, and in general leads to a happy loosening-up of staid attitudes. And it is joyful and optimistic. The result is a style of liturgy which many people have found helpful. Celebrants have learned to be more relaxed, everyone feels they are involved and have a part to play. This raises the question of diffusion. All this sounds—and is—very different from what is normally met with in most parishes on a Sunday. Is this something élitist, the affair of just a few? Up till recently, one might have been tempted to think so; but a number of recent events lead one to suppose otherwise. There is the sustained popularity, for example, of a large prayer-group with Mass which meets regularly in Westminster Cathedral. More important, there have been a number of significant conferences, both in Ireland and in England. Attendance has been numbered in hundreds and even thousands. Recently at Manchester, for instance, 450 priests took part. This, for England, is something extremely unusual. The liturgies were immensely moving: simple, dignified, prayerful, joyful. Not every prayer-group need, of course, be charismatic. The sheer experience of praying together almost inevitably alters one's understanding and expectations of the liturgy. And in this connection it is heartening to learn that a recent estimate puts the number of practising Catholics in the United States who already belong to some form of prayer-group at one in a hundred. England cannot yet match that figure, and it is too early yet to say how the Charismatic Renewal will develop over here. But already it has made a considerable impact, not least among the clergy. It may well turn out to provide one answer to what is perhaps the most commonly voiced complaint today—the attitude of priests towards the liturgy.

Such a complaint stems from expectations which are being frustrated: this in turn results from two differing conceptions of the liturgy and of the role of the ministerial priesthood. One, basing itself on key passages in the Council documents, looks for an increasing measure of active lay participation. The other leans on an older, at times one-sided and even mechanical view of the sacraments. It sees the role of the priest as all-important, and interprets active participation as something essentially interior. It was inculcated in training, along with a worthy but old-fashioned seminary piety summed up in the phrase 'My Mass'. This whole clerical spirituality was reinforced by the daily experience of celebrating devoutly in a style which took little notice of the congregation. Many good and sincere men undoubtedly find it difficult to change their attitude or their manner of celebrating, and to this extent it is certainly right to speak of the abiding influence of preconciliar theology and training. From the point of view of the laity, this is unfortunate. A tension exists in many parishes, but it can be met at its most acute in convents and schools. It is necessary to examine the influence that these institutions are beginning to have on the liturgical life of the country.

Schools

Nuns have in general taken more kindly to renewal than have their male counterparts or indeed most priests. This may be because they had more ground to make up. Even so, the way that they have set about studying and implementing the Council documents puts the men to shame. The enthusiasm may at times have been a trifle uncritical, but there is no doubting the achievement, embarrassing as it may be for us as priests to admit it. For the fact is that many nuns (and many of the laity too) are now theologically aware and articulate. As a result of courses, retreats, programmes of renewal at Rome and elsewhere abroad as well as at home, they now have expectations of the liturgy which are not always met. How long their traditional kindness and respect for the priest will continue to protect him from open criticism is a moot point. Where the pastoral needs of their pupils are concerned, teaching religious tend to be more exacting than they would be in the case of their own personal needs. This brings us to the issue of liturgy in schools, which is rendered particularly complex by the often large numbers of pupils at different levels of maturity.

In the past, the norm was generally a single Mass attended—often under compulsion—by the whole school. Increasingly it is being recognized that Class Masses or Year Masses are far more suitable, as this enables the children to be more involved and at their own level. Some schools (why only some?) are fortunate enough to have a full-time chaplain. Where daily Mass is celebrated, it is usually on a voluntary basis, during free time. Whether for large groups or for small, such school Masses are usually well prepared, with the children choosing readings, composing prayers, arranging the room or chapel with flowers, posters, banners and other work. There is usually enthusiastic and well-rehearsed singing, and an increasing use, for special occasions, of movement and drama: nevertheless, these observations tend to be truer of primary schools than of secondary schools and of girls than of boys. Then there are the tremendous opportunities, especially for older pupils, afforded by weekend retreats, days of recollection held away from school in the welcoming environment of a retreat-house, and often continued afterwards in prayer-groups. All this is probably best summed up by the one word *experience*—of prayer and of liturgy. There is thus a generation of Catholics growing up with an experience of liturgy that was not always available to their parents. With this experience comes an expectation, sometimes expressed in apparently negative terms. 'The parish Mass is boring. Father doesn't sound as though he means it.' In some regrettable cases, a hiatus does seem to exist between school and parish. For the most part, however, staff and priests together are beginning to rise to the great challenge presented by the Directory on Masses with Children. As with the charismatic movement, so with school liturgies. The experience of attending or celebrating can have a great influence on one's understanding and appreciation of the liturgy. Sensitivity to the needs of children—something all good priests should have in their bones—now becomes an education for the celebrant. To give an extreme example: one diocesan chaplain to the mentally-handicapped admits that he has learned more about the liturgy from serving the mentally-handicapped than from anything else in his life.

We have spoken at length, and in rather glowing terms, about liturgy in schools. Where can adults turn to for a living liturgy that supports and builds up faith, especially as the atmosphere they live in is increasingly unhelpful to that faith? There is our old friend the Summer School—not just that of the SSG but those of the many similar organizations that run catechetical and theology courses, Catholic people's weeks, study-days, and so forth. Many participants find here a vision of the liturgy, and of the Church as community, which sadly eludes them in the parish. Then there is the work of the many retreat-houses and pastoral centres. All these provide further opportunities for many Catholics to experience and benefit from a style of liturgy which ordinary parishes at present find it harder to supply. But when all this is said and done, what of the majority who have not the time or money to tap these resources? In a small number of parishes, the attempt has been made to initiate a full-blown programme of renewal based on charismatic principles.[2] More commonly, liturgical committees are being formed which, at their best, help the parish priest to keep in touch with his parishioners' differing needs and aspirations, besides assisting him in preparing the actual celebrations. House Masses and small group Masses have been found extremely effective in enabling Catholics of all ages and levels to experience the Eucharist in a more intimate setting which both deepens their understanding of the Mass and builds up a spirit of community. It is sometimes possible to focus such a celebration around a sick parishioner who is unable to attend Mass regularly. The revised rites of weddings, funerals and baptisms can provide other occasions for a liturgy that touches the realities of life in a more personal manner.

Other influences

So far, we have emphasized the contribution from Europe and America in helping us implement the revisions initiated by Rome. What of influences from further afield or nearer home? Among European countries, England enjoys a privileged position in the ecumenical field; but, despite the welcome improvement in relations at all levels, inter-Church influence has had little effect on our liturgy. The wide experience of the Free Churches in extempore prayer and dynamic preaching has hardly been drawn upon. Nor has the language of the Prayer Book. The Anglican musical tradition? Insofar as this is best exemplified in the great cathedrals, it is a choral and non-participatory (or, at least, congregationally passive) style of celebration. One thing, though, that we have drawn upon with gratitude is the magnificent heritage of English hymns. Otherwise, the non-catholic Churches have been faced with very similar problems to those of ourselves, and have—if anything—been in debt to Catholic practice and experience—although this must be said very tentatively and without complacency.

Influences from further afield? From the Church in the Third World? There seems little doubt that the numerical centre of gravity in Catholicism has moved away from Europe and that the process is irreversible, at least in the foreseeable future. Before long, this is bound to have a quite unpredictable effect on the liturgy in Asia, Africa and Latin America. What repercussions might we expect in Europe? Nothing very direct. The *Missa Luba*, for example, was popular as a record; but, so far as I know, it was never sung live in an English church. This is not surprising, since the more a liturgical style is suited to a non-European environment the less it is likely to suit Europe. However, our growing awareness of worldwide liturgical diversity—and of unity within this diversity—ought to make us more tolerant of local variations at home. And what of providing liturgies specifically for immigrants? There is another potential source of influence from the Third World in the shape of the increasingly important movement represented by Liberation Theology. Writers like Segundo and Gutierrez are trenchant in their criticisms of the 'bank-balance approach to the Mass', or to what they term 'sacramental intoxication'. They express a serious reminder that the liturgy, even the revised liturgy, is never an end in itself. It is meant to build up a Christian community that is so in more than name: men and women conscious of their mission to the world in which they live, and whose message of love gains credibility from their commitment both to care for individuals and to the wider demands of social justice. The full impact of these authors has yet to be felt. We are perhaps more ready to listen to critics from nearer home.

A number of books evaluating the progress of the liturgy since the Council have recently appeared on both sides of the Atlantic. Crichton's *The Once and the Future liturgy*[3] and Gelineau's *The Liturgy Today and Tomorrow*[4] are merely two of the best-known. A certain consensus is emerging. The new liturgy has its faults. As it is being implemented, if not in its conception, it is too wordy and didactic. More attention must be given to silence, to music, to non-verbal forms of communication. Prayer must not be stifled. There is a pressing need for smaller group-liturgies to supplement the ordinary parish community; need, too, for celebrations on a 'cosmic' scale, with the use of richer, more festive resources from time to time. One of the greatest dangers facing the new liturgy is seen to be a form of neo-rubricism, the timid or lazy settling into a familiar and undemanding rut. And, alas, the familiar complaint about the quality of celebrants.

Some of these criticisms tally in a remarkable manner with those voiced by small but influential groups concerned to preserve the Latin or improve the quality of the English used in the liturgy. Such an attitude is not to be confused with that of extremists who abominate the new liturgy along with the Council which begat it. No, it betokens a serious concern for important values. If it is true that decisions about the liturgy should be taken on pastoral rather than purely aesthetic grounds, it is also true that beauty is an aid to prayer. A sense of mystery, of reverence for God's majesty, are still needed in worship; and we do well to be reminded of this. Because Latin can contribute in this respect, and because it is also a powerful (but not the only) symbol of universality, it will never disappear completely; although its use in the future seems bound to be somewhat limited. Few adult Catholics would now wish to put the clock back, and fewer still of the young who have never known an all-Latin liturgy. The biggest single influence in the liturgical life of this country since the Council has been, quite simply, the sheer experience of being able to celebrate and pray the Mass in English.

Notes

1   Indeed, for much of ICEL's existence, England has been over-represented on the panel of translators by comparison with other countries outside Great Britain.

2   See J. Koenig in the *Clergy Review*, July 1978.

3   Veritas Publications, Dublin, 1978.

4   Darton, Longman and Todd, 1978.

8 Into the Melting-Pot:
Pointers towards a New Liturgical Music
Nicholas Kenyon

This will not be a chapter of prognostications or prophecies; it will provide simply a collection of disparate clues to the future. We are too close to the experiences of the last fifteen years to be able to construct one of those helpful statistical graphs which, by the simple expedient of extrapolating a line or curve, gives a supposedly reliable guide to the world's population in the year 2000, or the cost-of-living index in the week after next. Besides, nobody would pretend that the story of liturgical music in this country since Vatican II could be illustrated by a single line or a single curve. A host of conflicting influences has determined the course of events which was detailed in a previous chapter by John Ainslie, and here I shall do no more than pick out a few which may influence the development of liturgical music in this country during the coming years.

Polarities

The conscientious church musician who followed current thinking and public debate about liturgical music in the years following the Council could be forgiven if, by the early 1970s, he was developing a disease which felt like acute schizophrenia. He was being pulled in different directions by forces which, if they were not actually opposed, certainly appeared so; and both forces claimed his loyalty with special insistence. There were countless versions of both views; I have chosen two which set the matter in stark perspective.

The conventional attitude, elegantly expressed in the correspondence columns of the quality press and repeated with weary disillusion by many choir-trainers, was that in the reformed liturgy the Church had abandoned her cultural heritage. A foremost proponent of that view was the then Master of Music at Westminster Cathedral, Colin Mawby. In a talk broadcast on BBC Radio 3 in March 1972 devoted to the changes in the liturgy of Holy Week and their musical implications, entitled *The New Reformation*, he said that the Church has, to a large extent, alienated its serious musicians over the last few years...

'a musician feels as if his birthright has been sold for a mess of poor, vernacular pottage'. He talked of 'the abolition of so much church music', of young people 'who bitterly resent the fact that they are being denied the right to enjoy the musical and cultural heritage of Catholicism', and he reached the conclusion that 'we undoubtedly have a very serious responsibility to keep the music of the Church available in its correct surroundings and pass on to future generations the cultural heritage of Catholicism'.

This notion of the liturgy as the framework for a 'cultural heritage' which Catholics have 'a right to enjoy' was a potent one, and it expressed blatantly what other musicians had only dared to hint at: that the form of the liturgy was there simply to serve the music for which it provided a fitting framework. Change was permissible so long as it did not interfere with this inherited edifice. The musician was not there to serve the liturgy: on the contrary, he had a 'birthright', consisting presumably of all the great music ever written for the celebration of the Church's liturgy throughout history, which he had to protect against the danger of its 'abolition.'

Through such strongly-articulated views as these, the cause of those who wished to preserve the liturgical music of the past became inextricably linked to the cause of those who resented change in the liturgy (or rather mandatory change, for the argument always went: 'let those who want change, change, but let us also have the right to preserve the past as it is'). The traditional choirmaster was therefore faced with an acute dilemma: in the face of such dissatisfaction from the musical authority in the highest church in the land, was it not his duty to hold out for as much of the music he and his choir 'performed' in the old liturgical framework? Would not anything else, any compromise with the 'vernacular pottage', be a betrayal of the cultural heritage which he held in trust for future generations?

At the same time as this approach to musical change was on the one hand being taken as accepted truth by the media and by many secular musicians, and on the other being totally ignored by those parishes which went about the work of liturgical renewal without the help of a choir, a completely different perspective was also being presented. This was the radical criticism of the new Order of Mass which came from those whose liturgical thought had been opened up by the remarkable opportunities for adaptation and freedom within liturgical forms given in principle, and with safeguards, by the Constitution on the Liturgy. That document's statements on this matter can still seem remarkable, especially against the background of book-following rubricism which so often passes for liturgy in this country: 'Even in the liturgy, the Church has no wish to impose a rigid uniformity in matters which do not implicate the faith or the good of the whole community; rather does she respect and foster the genius and talents of the various races and nations....' (art 37). 'Provision is to be made, when revising the liturgical books, for legitimate variations and adaptations to different groups, regions, and peoples....' (art 38). 'The rites should be distinguished by a noble simplicity; they should be short, clear, and unencumbered by any useless repetitions...' (art 34). The possibilities inherent in these statements had been explored in this country (one thinks of the work of the Pratts, and of Sebastian Moore and Kevin Maguire in Liverpool), but the expression of them which came home with particular force to those church musicians able to be present was that which dominated the first meeting in England of the international church music group, Universa Laus. This took place at Wood Hall, Leeds, over a mere weekend (2-4 November 1973), and for the first time it brought English-speaking musicians into contact with some of the most adventurous thought from the Continent.

So far from viewing the new Order of Mass as a revised set of rubrics into which the church musicians had to insert pieces of music, it was made evident that it was regarded only as a blueprint. It was Père Gelineau who put the attitude most concisely when he talked of the new order as 'a ball which we have been thrown. Can we make of it a living liturgy?' He stressed the need not simply to accept every detail of what had been proposed. 'We are not being critical enough about certain sections, for instance the responses, which are simply ineffective, ... we must discover a living communication based on the fundamental parts of the liturgy.' Bernard Huijbers said that his experience in Amsterdam had lead to the same conclusion: 'We were one of those places which anticipated the official Vatican approval of the vernacular... we simplified the *Ordo* by eliminating many small phrases we felt had lost their meaning... this had the effect of enhancing the major building blocks of the liturgy... the sequence of musical forms no longer had such a marked obligatory character. One may ask whether such deletion did not run the risk of losing the very substance of the traditional liturgy. In fact our experience was quite the opposite: it gave us a growing clarification of the meaning of the heart of the liturgy.' Huijbers' moral was put with typical frankness: 'We have found the new order unhelpful to say the least... it prescribes feelings, prepackaged, so that a community can hardly keep pace, let alone make them their own... I regret that the makers of the new order have exempted themselves and the new local leaders from the task of remaking liturgy over and over again.' Well, perhaps not all local leaders were as ready as Huijbers to accept that responsibility; but the question of whether they had the right to do so was clearly put by Gelineau: 'How much permission do we have? It is important that communities should show signs of communion with each other, but this is through confessing the same faith and *not* by using the same material forms of expression... it is obvious that different hierarchies exercise their roles in different ways in different parts of the Church... the answer is, as ever, in the ancient tradition of the Church and the documents of Vatican II... the liturgy will not have any real life until each culture and (speaking carefully) each community gives it its expression. It is in that sense that the reform is a ball which has been thrown at us for our response.'

For the musician, the logical conclusion of that view was almost as disconcerting as that of Mr Mawby's. Liturgical music had to start, if the anti-musical metaphor may be allowed, from scratch. All certainties as to how music slotted into the liturgy were removed, especially since that liturgy had to reflect the individual community and its state of awareness and responsiveness. Of course, this was a perfectly orthodox view. The General Instruction on the Roman Missal, promulgated in April 1969, had said that 'the pastoral effectiveness of a celebration depends in great measure on choosing readings, prayers and songs which correspond to the needs, spiritual preparation and attitudes of the participants'. (But then that document, though published with the revised missal was, shockingly, not made available in separate form in England until the Catholic Truth Society issued it more than four years later, at the end of 1973.) The implications for the church musician were bewildering. On what sure ground could he build the future?

Straws in the wind

Among the plethora of people's Masses, hymns in idioms so nicely characterized by Elizabeth Poston as 'the pop, the plush and the twee', and other assorted pieces of publishing exploitation, there was precious little in those uncertain years after the introduction of singing in the vernacular which actually gave positive hope or guidance to the musician caught between the prevailing intolerancies—as illustrated in John Ainslie's second chapter (pp. 96 ff.) It points, too, to the fundamental difficulty we encountered in those years, which was isolated by John Michael East in his address to the 1978 Universa Laus Congress—we lacked in this country any indigenous tradition of

Catholic music-making and composition on which to build. And we did not treat it as a priority to create one. 'We have been looking for blooms where we have sown no seeds.'

In 1972, I ran a small questionnaire in a column on music in the magazine of the Catholic Missionary Society, the *Catholic Gazette*—not a publication read by specialist musicians, but one that evidently reached many clergy and parishioners involved in music. The results were not statistically relevant; they provide no analyses to compare with those from the Portsmouth and Liverpool dioceses mentioned earlier. But the comments were revealing: they showed a preoccupation with the business of 'getting people to sing' that made it clear that this was the one musical feature of liturgical reform which had actually taken root in this country. Whether it was hymns (usually), pop Masses (quite often), conventional Ordinary settings (rarely) or new psalms and responses (almost never) scarcely mattered. Success or failure was easy to judge: 'I am very dissatisfied. If only the people would sing and enjoy it.' 'The PP is loath to push anything.' 'The priest should keep on at the congregation to sing.' 'Congregational singing was introduced by the last PP and he encouraged it, but so far it has not been mentioned by the new one.' Small wonder that judgements on new developments and old losses were confused: 'I like the Latin Mass and hope that in the future we will sing it more often (age 14)'. On pop Masses: 'Older generation divided in response depending on whom they talked to and whether grandchild sang a solo. No musical or liturgical objections raised, only emotional.'

There were, however, straws in the wind: isolated incidents and publications which pointed, if not directly forward, then at least somewhere in the distance between the polarities. One extraordinary early effort which completely misfired deserves to be mentioned here. Early in 1969 (even before the introduction of the new Order of Mass, that is), Burns and Oates announced a most ambitious publishing programme, *Celebrating the Presence of the Lord*. It was initially to be adapted directly from the Dutch products of Huijbers, Oosterhuis and their collaborators; it was presented with very little change. In a remarkably optimistic specimen leaflet, the liturgy for Whit Sunday was given not only with the music and texts of new songs, but also with a complete alternative unofficial liturgy. One of Oosterhuis's eucharistic prayers was provided, for example, with the Roman Canon printed opposite in small type as an optional substitute. Not only were the prayers not approved; the whole idea of freedom in this area had not been previously raised. Whether anyone at Burns and Oates seriously thought that this would be tolerated remains unclear. By

September 1969, what were euphemistically described as 'various discussions with the National Liturgical Commission' had resulted in the abandonment of the 'unofficial' texts, and long delays in printing the music. Two recordings of the songs were issued which demonstrated all too well how strange they would sound when sung by a conventional English choir. The whole project soon collapsed, and there ended one of the most adventurous attempts to introduce continental liturgical thinking 'neat' into this country.

Such progress as there was towards flexibility and rethinking came unexpectedly, and sometimes with dubious results. It was a measure of the complete ineffectiveness of the National Liturgical Commission and its music section (which, as in the previous example, acted only rarely, and then usually negatively) that its approval-mechanism for new music dropped out of use so quickly; it had succeeded in laying down no positive guidelines and had encouraged no talent. Yet accepting for a moment the necessity of censors, should they not have had a look at the most interesting setting of the Ordinary of the Mass which appeared in 1971, that by Gordon Rock, called *A Pilgrim's Mass*, published by Mayhew-McCrimmon? Here was adaptability in action; the Mass was a genuine product of a community (at least, of that gathered for a weekend course) and all the texts of the Ordinary had been rewritten to fit into metrical frameworks for singing. Some of the results were alarming. The Creed was reduced to such banal declarations as 'I believe the church is holy, I believe the church is true, / I believe the church was made for all men, not just me and you'. The line 'showed us all the way to heaven' was provided with an alternative in a footnote (presumably for those who didn't like the idea of heaven) 'showed us life goes on for ever'; and there was an instruction that Verse 6 which 'is meant to sum up the proper reaction to doubts which assail us' could be prefaced by 'an interlude in which people voice significant dilemmas, such as "Why am I a spastic?" to a quiet musical background'. That left (and leaves) one speechless; nevertheless, here for the first time in published form in this country was an Ordinary in which the texts and their functions had been rethought and rewritten to create a 'local liturgy'. Like other straws in the wind, it blew away; its impetus was not maintained,

If there was an experimental tradition in post-conciliar liturgical music in this country which had any continuity at all, then it was undoubtedly to be found in such annual meetings as the Low Week course of the Church Music Association and the summer schools of the Society of St Gregory. What they achieved during isolated weeks had to be maintained during the rest of the year by the written debate and discussion of the societies' magazines: the incomparably lively and outspoken *Church Music*, edited by Bill Tamblyn, and the supremely well-informed and weighty *Liturgy*, later *Life and Worship*, edited by J.D. Crichton and then by Frank Thomas and Christopher Walsh. But these were no substitute for the practical work of the courses, for which a host of new pieces were written for use in liturgies on which creative effort, thought, time, trouble and prayer had all been expended. The annual doses of inspiration and example which these provided for an all-too-small body of church musicians cannot be overvalued. There was little, deliberately, that could be transported directly back to parishes and schools—though Michael Dawney's now well-known setting of the ICET Gloria was commissioned for an SSG summer school, and many other small works have been successfully transplanted. But the mind goes back to pieces which gave uniquely fruitful examples of what was possible: Bill Tamblyn's settings of the Proper for Easter Wednesday and Thursday, for the 1969 CMA week; the elaborate settings of Christopher Walker for the SSG summer schools in the mid-1970s; the highly practical acclamations of Philip Duffy; the psalm-settings of Laurence Bévenot and Charles Watson—here, if anywhere, was a new liturgical music in the making.

Two large-scale works of recent years put this progress in more tangible form: both showed, in very different ways, what a single skilled composer working in the established tradition of the creative artist in the liturgy, could make of the framework of the new Mass. The annual Music Week at Spode House, Staffordshire, produced in 1974 perhaps the single most impressive work for the new liturgy. This was Robert Sherlaw Johnson's *Festival Mass of the Resurrection*, a highly imaginative and dramatically-conceived work; it mixed Latin and English texts in an elaborate processional Introit, which mingled the journey to the empty tomb with the lighting of the paschal candle; it provided simple congregational responses and ministerial chants unified by simple accompaniments, a troped Kyrie (with English tropes, but the refrain in Greek), and a vivid Latin Gloria setting, with accompaniment for organ, tam-tam and bells. The most important thing about Sherlaw Johnson's challenging work was that it used a distinctively modern, coherent musical idiom. There was no apology for a 'sacral style', yet, permeated as it was by a profound sense of ritual, the simplicity of the responses did not jar in any way with the uncompromising musical content of the rest. It demanded highly professional musical forces, but it involved everyone.

Bill Tamblyn's *ICEL Mass*, completed in August 1975 and revised in January 1976, was something different. His brief from the International Committee on English in the Liturgy was to compose a musically-linked setting of all the ordinary parts of the Mass in the new text. Tamblyn, making no apology for his eclecticism and saying that 'there are no prizes for composer-spotting' was as contemporary as Sherlaw Johnson, but drew together a vast range of styles around some essentially very simple material. He chose as the dramatic pivot of his setting the Acclamation after the Consecration: from one four-note phrase and one five-note phrase presented here he derived much of the musical material for the Mass. The whole setting began on the note G at the start of Mass, grew away from that tonal centre, and moved back towards it for the conclusion and dismissal at the end of the celebration. The setting made explicit the structure of the liturgy and the relationship between its constituent parts in a way that no other had succeeded in doing up to this time. It demanded no mean skill on the part of the celebrant; a good organist; and some quite complex leadership from a solo cantor and unison choir.[1]

A future for the past

But where did we leave the choir? Defending its cultural heritage. One of the problems with the more adventurous developments such as those outlined above was that all too often they had to take place without the assistance and skilled support of choirs. Instead of attempting to find a new role in accordance with the liturgical documents of the Council and after, too many choirs had retreated into a position of retrenchment. After a first flurry of activity, even the provision of traditionally-conceived choral Ordinaries in English from the publishing houses dried up: there was clearly no demand for them. Yet the choirs were, in many cases, still there.

So the most pressing single practical problem in reconciling the polarities demonstrated at the start of this chapter and in creating a worthy new liturgical music had become evident: it was to persuade the skilled musicians of the Church that they had a vital role to play in the musical renewal of the liturgy. But this required a radical reappraisal of the choir's role: a willingness not merely to defend an aesthetic repertoire, but to open their work to criticism. It was clear, on the one hand, that the music of the past had an enormous amount to contribute to a renewed liturgy—for it had not lost the power to communicate powerfully the meaning of the words it set. On the other hand, though, it was also clear that some of what was traditionally regarded as the choir's repertoire might now be thought unsuitable for use in the liturgy. The dilemma of the liturgically-sensitive musician in this situation was most honestly and clearly expressed by a musically-sensitive liturgist, J. D. Crichton, in an important talk, 'liturgy in a dechristianized world', given to the Spode House Music Week in 1966: 'It is not that I dislike plainsong and polyphony. I have lived with both since I can remember anything about music at all. If I were consulting my purely personal tastes there is a great deal of the plainsong corpus which I would wish to retain because I do not know of anything better as a vehicle of worship. I can sit entranced listening to the great polyphony of the past... but both are less than perfect when they obscure the message either by attracting one's attention to the music itself or by making the words unintelligible... Many is the monastic church I have sat in vainly hoping to discern the words that were being poured out in a torrent of square notes...'.

Music for the new liturgy (though indeed the same should have been true of the old liturgy) must be intelligible and suited to its function. As the American Bishops put it in their document *Music in Catholic Worship:* 'The musician with a sense of artistry and a deep knowledge of the rhythm of the liturgical action will be able to combine the many options into an effective whole.... He must enhance the liturgy with new creations... and with those compositions from the time-honoured treasury of sacred music which can serve today's celebration...'.

This in its turn required an abandonment of old certainties about the worth of all liturgical music which had been accepted as such in the past. It meant subjecting each piece of plainsong or polyphony to the same criteria of appropriateness as might be applied to a folk Mass. Of course, some historically-aware musicians had already begun to question the blanket acceptance of all church music of the past which fell into the magic categories of plainsong or polyphony. As early as December 1965, Anthony Milner demonstrated the flimsy basis on which the idea of an identifiable corpus of this music rested in three articles in *The Month*. He pointed out that modern musicology had made available a large amount of church music never performed by choirs, who touched 'barely one-thousandth part of it'; he identified the special importance given to Palestrina and the Roman School as a product of the nineteenth century, particularly of the work of Biani and the Papal Choir; and he insisted that 'so-called tradition reveals many features of dubious value and little antiquity'. These attacks could be written off as just another example of reformist destructiveness; what they raised on a much broader plane, however, was the problem behind the apparent consensus about the idiom for church music in an age when certainties had been removed,

An idiom for church music

No discussion revealed more clearly latent attitudes to the liturgical music of the future than that of idiom: is there such a thing as church music, and if so how do we recognize it? Superficially there was a new post-conciliar answer, expressed with clear sense by that splendid fence-sitting document, *Musicam sacram:* 'No kind of sacred music is prohibited from liturgical actions by the Church as long as it corresponds to the spirit of the liturgical celebration and the nature of its individual parts.' So, speaking purely musically, anything goes as long as it fits: *Plaisir d'amour, Godspell* or *Orbis factor.* But clearly there was more to it than this, for the acceptance that some music is suited for use in church and some is not runs very deep. (Just try imagining Rachmaninov's Second Piano Concerto in church—though worse things have, I expect, been heard.)

The consensus of the Roman documents since the *Motu proprio* of Pius X in 1903 had begun to fade somewhat, signalling a considerable change of attitude. Pius X demanded three characteristics of 'sacred music': 'In the first place, holiness and goodness of form; from these comes its other quality of universality.' To this was added the notion that 'it must be holy'. No attempt was made to define these qualities in musical terms: it was enough to say that the traditional music of the church possessed them. The argument was circular. These statements were repeated in the 1955 decree, *Musicae Sacrae Disciplina,* but with a marked lack of emphasis on universality, for many exceptions in this field had already been permitted. In the Constitution on the Liturgy (n. 116), with its profoundly pastoral approach to music, direct instruction had been reduced to 'The Church acknowledges Gregorian Chant as specially suited to the Roman liturgy; therefore, *other things being equal* [my italics], it should be given pride of place in liturgical functions.'

The thinking embodied in Pius X's document was a product of nineteenth-century attitudes to the music of the past, and it placed itself in the tradition of a theory about the function of music in worship which went back to the Council of Trent. Trent had declared: 'in the Masses which are celebrated with singing and with organ, let nothing profane be intermingled, but only hymns and divine praises. The singing should be arranged not to give empty pleasure to the ear but in such a way that the words may be understood by all, and thus the hearts of the listeners be drawn to the desire of the heavenly harmonies, in the contemplation of the joys of the blessed.' And in the same century Thomas Morley said that church music should 'bind the ears of the listener as it were in chains of gold to the contemplation of heavenly things.'

Such a directly transcendental approach would clearly not survive the idea of a liturgy which worshipped an immanent, not merely a remote, God. And there were other problems associated with the traditional assumptions about what constituted church music, which were being raised forcefully by continental theorists. To some of them, the use of plainsong and polyphony served only to reinforce a feeling of cultural well-being and certainly—it tells us where we are, so the argument went, and it tells us that everything's fine. Gino Stefani put this strongly in *Concilium,* February 1969: 'The reception of art... under certain conditions fosters a sense of socio-religious belonging.... Such music is not part of the action of the assembly or of any of its members; it is instead part of the atmosphere or the order of the architecture.... It is good to cultivate art; it is good to frequent the church. Every civilized person and every cultured man does so! The implication of this reassuring and middle-class type of reception are: the liturgy as a *locus* of culture... Catholic triumphalism...'.

As so often, it was Père Joseph Gelineau who had already provided a direction out of this impasse, in his magnificent book *Voices and Instruments in Christian Worship* (written, it should be remembered, before the Constitution on the Liturgy, though translated into English only after the Constitution was published). 'Is there not a style specially fitted for liturgical use?... It seems generally accepted, yet the idea may well be disputed... It would be a gross mistake to think that one is producing something sacred or Christian just by building in the Romanesque style or by composing in the style of Palestrina.' Yet this was, of course, precisely what people did think. They aimed at a particular style, and were able to justify the appalling results—the Mass of St Cecilia by Dom J. Egbert Turner OSB or Kitson in D—by turning to Sir Richard Terry's *reductio ad absurdum* of this sacral idiom argument: 'The actual merits of any music written for the Church are of secondary importance to its character. This would appear so obvious that it seems superfluous to mention it...' (*Catholic Church Music,* p. 51).

Gelineau continues: 'If a style is sacred, this can only be because it signifies what is transcendent in the sphere of religion... a specific quality is not to be sought for in perceptible forms that can be particularized and assigned to material elements.' That is to say, it is the use, function and significance of music which distinguishes it, not whether it is written in a 'churchy' style; insofar as it is the servant of the words and of the liturgical action, then it is 'sacred'. Such a view does not contradict the view of the papal documents: indeed it supports them to the extent that plainsong, for example, provides a prime example of music which signifies its purpose in its content. But Gelineau's formulation broadens the scope of the papal pronouncements (as they had been gradually broadening themselves over the years) to admit any music to the liturgy which communicates these qualities. Moreover, it steers us carefully between any notion that church music can be regarded as pure 'art for art's sake', and the idea that the trivial and the unworthy are valid if they are appropriately 'sacral' in style. It relies on the integrity of the individual composer, and provides no easy answers.

So how is today's composer to respond to the music around him in creating a new liturgical music? In England he has a country whose latent, dormant notions of church music probably consist of 'Abide with me' and Mendlessohn's *Wedding March*. He has the example of *Godspell* and *Jesus Christ Superstar* to help or confuse him with fashionable notions of what an up-to-date religious idiom might be (though how fascinating to note that a hit-song from Andrew Lloyd Webber's more recent *Evita* returns to a consciously archaic, organum-like church style in its cries of 'Salve regina, mater misericordiae'). He has a popular style, measured on a scale starting from Radio 1 and plumbing the depths of the Eurovision Song Contest, created by commercial pressures, linked to the dissemination of values on the media which he may well not wish to reflect. He has, perhaps, the remnants of an English folk-song tradition—though how far that is still a continuous living tradition outside the collections of Cecil Sharp and Vaughan Williams is debatable. And finally, he has that whole myriad of conflicting, interacting styles known only to a tiny proportion of the population, which go under the heading of 'contemporary music'. Here the most adventurous developments of the day undoubtedly take place, but whether because they are fifty years ahead of their time, or because (as the composer Edgard Varèse insisted) the public is fifty years behind the times, they have not yet acquired the power to communicate instantly and clearly to the world around them.

One step enough

The current perspective on the future of church music was well summed up in the papers given at the first congress of Universa Laus to be held in this country, which took place at Strawberry Hill in August 1978, in conjunction with Summer School of the Society of St Gregory. As at the earlier, much smaller meeting at Wood Hall in 1973, the English tradition was challenged and stimulated by contributions from abroad. John Michael East's opening reflections on the lack of an indigenous, coherent Catholic tradition in this country have already been touched on, but his remarks on composers are highly relevant here. He made wry adaptations of two quotations to point up the English situation; first, quoting Pope Paul's address to his Cardinals on 23 June 1978, 'How many lay people... have assumed the place to which they are entitled in liturgical worship'—a remark which, he said, the late Pope intended as an exclamation, but which we in England might expect to be a question. And secondly, from Alec Robertson's book *Music of the Catholic Church* (1961): 'The composer of church music must be accorded freedom to write in the idiom of his time, as he does in secular music'—to which John East added: 'As things are now in this country, I think Fr Robertson will not quibble at my saying that the composer of church music must be accorded not only freedom but accorded encouragement.' However, and this was the crux of his talk, he insisted that we cannot abandon the effort to build a tradition simply because we do not have one to start from. We do not get round the problem by adopting some other tradition, for example in a 'pseudo-ecumenical' spirit, or by giving way to 'the temptation of expediency': we have to make a new tradition with those few materials which we have.

And speakers during the week echoed this theme. Eugenio Costa, drawing on a wide range of European examples, asked whether the liturgy and its music would draw together in the future: 'Will we be forced to deal with a progressive fragmentation of genres and styles, a growing bursting-apart-at-the-seams of church music? Or will we see a number of common traits emerging... and if this happens, will it be at a regional level, or a national level, or a continental or even a world-wide level? Will we be able to fix its laws?'

Helmut Hucke, summarizing many of the concerns about the nature of liturgical music which have been touched on in this chapter, isolated four different ways of looking at church music. First, as simply the musical contents contents of the liturgical books (but this meant in fact the 1903 *Editio Vaticana* as arranged by Solesmes!); second, as the sum of the repertoire written for use in the church's liturgy (the artistic heritage view); thirdly, as any music written in a so-called sacral style (church music as a specially holy sound); and fourth, church music as a function of the liturgical action—this last, he said, was the only supportable view, and in many ways the least restrictive.

But, as might have been anticipated, the most fundamental questioning of the role of music in the liturgy of the future came from Bernard Huijbers. He painted a picture of a Domkapellmeister who has achieved everything by way of reform in accordance with the spirit and the law of the church' documents, who has balanced the function of each sung part of the Mass in a perfect construction. But he feels that it all lacks reality: the liturgy, though splendidly reformed, has no contact with real life; 'the whole happening floats, loose from the earth, loose from the people...'. His talk was a plea for a liturgy grounded far more radically in present-day life, and less in those forms derived from the past. Music's function was important, but only insofar as the liturgy became less magical and ceased to 'abuse myth'.

It is a valuable warning. The structure of our liturgy must never be considered more important than its role of communication between man and God, or we shall revert to a situation in which it is the *content* of our liturgy which we prize rather than worship itself. There is already a new school of concert-liturgy, particularly in the United States, which has built magnificent monuments to man out of a vernacular choral liturgy; such massively-orchestrated (in all senses) examples as the work of C. Alexander Peloquin, which was 'toured' in 1977 to London and described by the composer to me as 'just like Wagner, *leitmotifs* and everything', produce on an unfamiliar congregation precisely the feeling of alienation Huijbers describes.

Yet I am sure that Huijbers overstates the case in wishing to destroy those forms of liturgy which link it to the past. The liturgy is essentially a historical act, and if belonging to a Catholic Church means anything at all, then it means unifying ourselves with those who in the past and in the future have carried out and will carry out the command to preach the Word and break bread. And the argument for the use of historical forms—for *not* relying, with arrogant confidence, purely on our own inspiration—has been well put by Huijbers' collaborator, Huub Oosterhuis. 'The liturgy', he wrote in *Prayers, Poems and Songs*,[6] gives us forms of expression when we ourselves are formless and uninspired.... Liturgy is discipline and faithfulness against the forgetfulness of time and boredom... a dedication to values which are always being forgotten, a practice in useless wisdom.... Liturgy is daring to use old words which we would not have thought of or found ourselves, words which have been handed down to us in an incalculably old tradition which is often dubious...'.

Exactly the same applies to music. The use of a piece of music, scribbled out yesterday or handed down for a thousand years, involves a reliance on someone else's expression of a shared faith. And that is what draws us together, and articulates our common relationship with God—whether we sing the music ourselves or make it ours as we listen. The more sensitively the music we use reflects the deepest concerns of those gathered together, the more precisely it matches the words, function and mood of the liturgical action, the more it helps to make concrete in one time and place *the eternal truths* which the liturgy embodies, so much more fully will music acquire that ministerial role, the *munus ministeriale* which the Church, recognizing its elemental power, grants it in the liturgy.

Notes

1   It ought to be mentioned that the ICEL Music Subcommittee, even after requesting (and getting) numerous modifications from the composer, still found the setting too strong for its weak stomach, and rejected it. The setting still exists, but has never been formally published.

9   Task Unfinished

Christopher J. Walsh

> Lord, as you give us the body and blood of your Son,
> guide us with your Spirit
> that we may honour you not only with our lips
> but also with the lives we lead.
>
> (*Roman Missal, 9th Sunday*)

For half a century the liturgical movement and for a whole decade the liturgical reform have busied themselves with the ways and means of honouring God with our lips. Latterly some welcome attention has been turned also to our hands and feet and eyes and ears. But our *lives*? Four years ago I wrote: 'True, every single text in the Roman liturgy will have been revised and translated, people will participate more evidently than they did twenty years ago, but the liturgy will be no more important and central to their lives than it was then, and the parish community will have no more sense of sharing, of mission, of transforming the world.... We have all the right words, books and formulae. What we need, however, is not texts but *communities*, real human communities of shared faith, shared concern, shared mission, shared celebration.'[1] As prophecies go, this was a fairly safe one. If anything, I see it as even truer and more urgent now than it was then, and in preparing a concluding chapter to this symposium, on the prospects for the future, I shall try to avoid futurology and to prophesy only in the original and unpopular sense of sounding warnings, unmasking illusions and pointing to the emperor's nakedness.

For to my mind the principal problem, indeed crisis, facing liturgy in this country is that of credibility. Despite all the revision and reform (and sometimes perhaps because of it), a hiatus amounting in many cases to a chasm of Grand Canyon proportions has opened up between language and experience, between description and reality, between ideology and fact. Thus: 'families' whose members know nothing of each other, 'communities' which are nothing of the sort, 'songs' which are recited, 'acclamations' which are muttered by one voice, baptisms where people are 'bathed' and 'buried' in Christ under 10ml of water and 'welcomed into a community' which has not bothered to turn up or even been informed of the event, 'meals' at which no one drinks and where 'sharing one bread' means simultaneous consumption of 500 individual breads, 'gifts of the people' which are not theirs and which they do not give, 'celebrations' which are the joyless and perfunctory discharge of an obligation. The list is depressing and almost infinitely extensible. It is questionable how long the liturgy can endure this corrupting disease without being irretrievably weakened. What is increasingly clear is that the condition can no longer, if it ever could, be rectified simply by adjustments to the words, actions and explanations of the liturgy. It is already beginning to look as if far too much attention and energy have been devoted to the words, rubrics and translations of the liturgy, which have been examined, revised, criticized and fought over almost in a vacuum of narcissistic introversion. Joseph Gelineau ends his recent book on the future of the liturgy wondering 'if the liturgy today is not more preoccupied with itself than with the Kingdom it proclaims'.[2] Reforms and revisions we have had in plenty, but liturgical *renewal* will never be achieved until our texts, rites and affirmations are translated not into this or that sort of English but into reality in the lived experience of the people; and they will rarely be experienced as real until the congregations celebrating them are genuine communities of faith, witness and action.

Such integral and integrated worship is not simply a fantasy; it shouts out to us from the Acts of the Apostles, the letters of St Paul, and the life of the early Church. Luke tells us that the earliest assemblies were devoted to the Apostles' teaching, to 'koinonia' (fellowship, sharing, distribution of goods), the breaking of bread and prayers (Acts 2:42). For St Paul, too, preaching the Gospel and sharing the Word, collecting money and sharing with the poor were acts of worship and as integral to the liturgy as prayer and sacrament. Evangelization brings faith and conversion, which result in thanksgiving and worship, which overflow in service of neighbour, which in turn reveals the love of God which inspires it, and evokes further faith and worship. And so on. Evangelization—worship—action constitute a cycle or spiral, each issuing from the other and provoking the next, each authenticating the other. It is striking that St Paul describes this whole spiral as 'liturgy' and 'service'.[3] For him, worship and apostolate are two poles of the one mystery by which the Church grows in the love which gave it birth and manifests to others the contagiousness of God's love and the impact of the Gospel. And the ensuing history of the Church in what de Lubac has called its period of 'explosive vitality' shows how it was not content simply to preach the gospel of love, but was determined to live it in organized and supportive brotherhood. Spontaneously it developed forms, realizations of this gospel which gave it expression and reality in inventive charity: collections, meals, distributions of food and clothing, relief services, shelter and hospitality, all of which were based in the Sunday assembly and found their goal and summit in it.[4] Loving service of neighbour is the principal authenticating sign of the presence and action of Christ. Christian community is built up and enlarged by its power. Liturgy promotes evangelization to the extent that worship expresses itself concretely in the effective charity of the community. The church, like Christ, exists to serve, and any departure from this vocation is a betrayal of its mission, a corruption of its witness. Jesus, after all, submitted his own preaching to verification in action: 'If you do not believe me, believe my works' (John 10:38). The Church can do no less.

But somewhere along the way we have broken the spiral. In our communities worship is demanded of everyone, but action and service is left to those who like that sort of thing or those we pay to do it in our name, and evangelization is virtually non-existent. Little by little, but alarmingly, attendance at the liturgy has become the only criterion of practice and expression of faith; all else is optional, supererogatory. Worse still, only one form of liturgy is offered and required, the Sunday Mass which, in its form, presupposes a prior catechesis which has not happened, full commitment which is not there, follow-up in action which does not materialize. In short, we have worshipping assemblies which are not communities of faith and action. And until they are, I do not believe the liturgy can ever be rehabilitated. It is imperative, therefore, that we recover the priority of evangelization and catechesis, develop a plurality of liturgical provision, and promote a reintegration of liturgy with service and social action. All that will demand, no doubt, a massive and radical change of pastoral strategy and practice, and a thoroughgoing reshaping, expansion and redeployment of ministry.[5]

Priority of evangelization and catechesis

For the majority of Catholics in this country, such evangelization and catechesis as they receive consists exclusively of a 7-10 minute homily at Sunday Mass, which is intrinsically incapable of bearing the weight put upon it. We have all experienced different preachers at different Masses each week selecting different readings for comment; whole books of the Bible that are (perhaps) read but never commented on;

major scriptural and theological themes that are avoided, trivialized or moralized upon; preaching suspended altogether for a pastoral letter or appeal of quite extraneous content, or because of summer heat or winter cold or the bus company's timetable or Father's holiday; sermons from the backs of envelopes, from the tops of heads, from the filing cabinet; diatribes, ferverinos, jeremiads, vapourizings, moralistic anecdotes. The Sunday homily is little short of a lottery, and lucky indeed is the congregation which hears the lectionary and its themes systematically and consistently expounded week by week over three, six, nine years. One understands why the call goes up in some quarters for a return to a syllabus of instruction, but given the heterogeneity of our congregations this would be equally unsuccessful. In any case, it is simply not the function of the homily, nor of the Mass liturgy as a whole, to evangelize and instruct. The Council recognized that 'the liturgy does not exhaust the entire activity of the Church.... Before men can come to the liturgy they must be called to faith and conversion.... Therefore the Church announces the good news of salvation to those who do not believe.... To believers also the Church must ever preach faith and conversion; she must prepare them for the sacraments, teach them to observe all that the Lord commanded, and encourage them to engage in all the works of charity, piety and the apostolate.'[6] Nowhere is it suggested or even envisaged that all this takes place during the Sunday Mass. Nor could it, given the diversity of situations, ages, religious development and commitment in a Sunday congregation. On the contrary, everything in the organization and texts of the Mass presupposes a level of belief, instruction and commitment which perhaps could be encountered in the days of Christendom, but which most certainly may not be presumed in our country today. How can the same few words, however conscientiously prepared and sensitively delivered, serve as appropriate instruction (and the only instruction) for school-children, sceptics, casual visitors, contemplatives, drifters, intellectuals, simple saints, the disturbed and distressed, reluctant teenagers, the uncommitted, the militant, who constitute the average assembly of the people of God on a Sunday morning? Jesus could hardly have managed it; we surely delude ourselves if we think we are coming near it.

Plurality of liturgical provision

At the moment we offer and require one single form of worship which, to make sense and satisfy, demands full sacramental participation, and for which thousands are simply not ready or willing.

Gelineau rightly remarks that 'it is just as unsatisfactory morally to oblige someone to attend a Eucharist if he does not want to go to communion as it is to deprive him of every part of the assembly because he does not yet feel up to taking part in the Lord's Supper'.[7] And we could add with equal justice that it is also as wrong to deprive many of the opportunity for deepening their faith and stretching their commitment by mediocre and undemanding celebrations as it is to pressurize the uncommitted into full sacramental participation when they are in no way ready for it.

The lately deceased eminent Paris pastoral theologian P.A. Liégé once wrote: 'It is important that the Church proposes the Eucharist to the faithful every Sunday, but there are baptized Christians for whom abstention from the Eucharist from time to time would be beneficial in order to revive their hunger; there are also baptized Christians whose situation is rather that of catechumenal development and for whom a non-eucharistic assembly would be more advisable; there are Christians for whom a weekly Eucharist exceeds the faith at their disposal and who could make better progress in the faith through non-eucharistic assemblies.... Is it not astonishing and scandalous to see certain groups of Christians whose faith is confessedly most uncertain rushing into celebrations of the Eucharist for which they are not disposed?'[8] Indeed, even committed believers might often benefit from a more subtle and varied rhythm of celebration and assembly, especially if they are not able to avail of group of celebrations or more homogeneous assemblies during the week.

The Church has been, perhaps understandably, slow to look seriously and self-critically at this issue, but pastoral reality and hard experience have already forced many to reconsider and discuss openly the related crisis in the celebration of other sacraments, notably admission to baptism and marriage, where it is increasingly recognized as irresponsible and intolerable to offer a sacrament when evidence of even the most basic faith, understanding and commitment is lacking; and yet no one is happy in the name of Christ simply to send people away empty-handed.

Reintegration of liturgy and action

'By this all men will know that you are my disciples, if you have love for one another' (John 13:55); 'I was hungry and you gave me food' (Mt 25:35); 'Go and tell John what you see and hear: the poor have the good news preached to them' (Mt 11:5). And yet 'practising Catholic' in our language does not mean one who manifests love, one who gives food to the hungry, one who brings good news to the poor of the earth, but one who goes to Mass on Sunday. Liturgy has been divorced from service, from witness, from its entire context. But service of God demands service of neighbour, communion with the Lord presupposes communion with our brothers. If the symbolism of shared bread is to achieve its full meaning as the means by which the body of Christ is built up, it must concretize itself in solidarity and re-distribution between rich and poor, inspired by God's love which we celebrate. The Eucharist cannot signify the banquet to which the Father invites the poor, the blind, the lame, when the community it brings together does not embody visibly, honestly and effectively the same concern.[9] Liturgy without service of neighbour destroys worship; it is that sacrifice without mercy which stinks in God's nostrils. We perhaps come nearer to admitting this in the case of the Church as an 'institution', but it is true of, and must be taken to heart by, the parish as a community and every individual within it. Refusal to par-ticipate actively in the liturgy is unacceptable, and communion by proxy unthinkable; is not a refusal to get actively involved in charit-able service equally unacceptable, leaving it to others to do it in our name equally unthinkable? A Mass-stipend does not absolve us from participation in the liturgy, no more than a money-offering discharges our Christian responsibility for the poor and oppressed. Giving of one's time, one's effort, one's self to the service of Christ's poor and the struggle for justice is not simply a permissible option for those who are temperamentally activist or politically inclined, which they are free to indulge as others might give themselves to bingo-calling, devo-tional sodalities, old-time dancing, or the parish football team. It is an obligation on every Christian; it is the one test of discipleship; and it derives from the liturgy, is inspired by it, and is inseparable from it.

Possibilities for action

Having eschewed all futurology, I could not now forecast the direction of future developments even if it were possible. But to compensate at least partially for the rather negative assessment of our present situa-tion, I would now like to point out what I see as seeds of promise already discernible, areas of possible development, action which could be taken immediately.

The most urgent need of all is for a rolling programme of formation in every locality. No one scheme, however well devised and staffed, could conceivably meet all the myriad needs, interests, gaps. But anything and everything which can assist any group or section in the local Church to grow in faith, understanding and commitment should be exploited, worked at, made more widely available, and co-ordinated, at least loosely, with all other local facilities. Already our efforts at adult formation extend from evening classes and weekend courses, through house-group discussions and prayer groups, to recollections and retreats. But talks and lectures are so often only one-off affairs on a topic of current concern—or a series promoted and planned for one parish only, rarely lasting more than a few weeks and generally reaching only the committed. House groups and prayer groups usually enjoy a longer life and greater continuity, but for want of an adequate long-term programme can often get becalmed and fail to make progress. There are agencies (like the FSA and the Grail) which produce discussion-materials for such groups, but we need far more of them producing far more schemes that will last a group not months but years and decades. And still we are likely to reach only the more articulate, literate and committed. A more comprehensive audience can undoubtedly be reached through pre-sacramental programmes of instruction which are already operating in some places. Couples seeking marriage, parents seeking baptism, first communion and confirmation for their children, can all be invited, cajoled or required to take part in preliminary instruction, which may, indeed should, extend far beyond the celebration of the sacrament and its consequences to almost any other aspect of faith and practice.[10]

Outside London, and perhaps some of the other conurbations, it is doubtful whether there are yet in this country sufficient numbers of unbaptized seeking baptism to warrant a full catechumenate like that restored in France a quarter of a century ago. Our greatest need now, and for a long time to come, is to provide catechesis not for the unbaptized who are not seeking it, but for the baptized who have never had it: those whose Christian formation ended, if it ever began, at eleven or fourteen; those who have never had the opportunity or the inclination to examine, consolidate or understand their inherited or married faith. Whatever the case with pre-baptismal catechumens, there is not a parish in the land which does not have an abundance of these post-baptismal catechumens. Sooner rather then later, every parish—or at least every town or deanery—must have a properly organized, permanent and systematically-worked-out programme of adult Christian formation, under whose umbrella provision can be made for all these different needs and circumstances. Only then will the Sunday homily be relieved of the impossible burden and expectations laid upon it; but, of course, we do not have to wait for the establishment of such a rolling programme before doing something about the homily. If it is to remain, even in the short term, as the principal vehicle of instruction then it must be rescued immediately from dissipation and ineffectuality by more conscientious planning and co-ordination: if all the priests of a place were to sit down together week by week and year by year to plan their homilies and preach on the same subjects, it would be an obvious but very welcome start.

Plurality of liturgical provision means the development of non-eucharistic and non-sacramental forms of worship, and according them proper recognition in the life of the Church. It sounds innocuous enough, but would probably demand a quite radical change of attitudes and habits. Elsewhere in the Church (e.g. widely in Latin America, increasingly in France[11]) non-eucharistic Sunday assemblies are already common. It is at least arguable that in this country at present we celebrate too many Sunday Masses, and until the number of priests falls rather more drastically (as it seems likely to do in the next fifteen years), it is unlikely that Church authorities will give much serious consideration either to alternative forms of Sunday assembly or to alternative sorts of ministry. But such developments should not be waited for fatalistically as expedients which cannot for much longer be avoided, but positively exploited as providential opportunities to get to grips with the questions of the deployment of existing clergy, the possibility of other forms of priesthood and ministry, and the need for other forms of worship and assembly.

Already we recognize that the Sunday parish Mass does not necessarily do children a lot of good, unless provision is made for their special needs. Sometimes this means entire Masses planned and celebrated primarily for them; at other times it means providing them with a simultaneous but separate Liturgy of the Word, differently constructed and conducted apart from that of the main assembly.[12] This is an important breach of the long-established principle of the unicity and universality of the Sunday assembly. Once breached, there are no logical reasons why such special provision should be limited to children, and plenty of pastoral reasons why it should be extended to the other groups and categories whose needs we discussed earlier. The case for a variety of 'entries' and 'exits' to the Sunday assembly, and for the development of other forms of celebration and of sharing the Word, has been convincingly argued and illustrated by Gelineau in his *The Liturgy Today and Tomorrow*.[13]

Sunday Mass is not the only instance, of course, where the Church seems to offer and demand all or nothing. In the wake of Catholics in France and Anglicans in England, priests have been forced not so much by reading as by pastoral experience to question the propriety of baptizing babies from families who not only do not 'practise' but whose faith is impossible to discern and whose understanding of a sacrament and its consequences is nil. While believing there is no proper basis for proceeding here and now with the sacrament, priests are yet reluctant to quench the burning flax and to repel a genuine approach to Christ and his Church, however weakly motivated. Latterly we have became equally uneasy about the ever-increasing number of baptized couples asking for marriage, where at least one and quite often both partners have a totally unformed faith and seemingly no conception of sacrament. But what else have we to offer?

The time has surely come for the Church to provide forms for the celebration of 'rites of passage' with those who wish to affirm the religious and Christian significance of these moments, but who lack the commitment appropriate for a sacrament. It is hard to see what objection there could be to a 'staged' celebration of baptism, whereby children could be welcomed, blessed and enrolled in a full liturgical celebration, but the actual baptism would be held over until such time as the families have received further catechesis and come to a better awareness of their responsibilities.[14] The case of marriage is canonically and theologically difficult, but there are strong pastoral and liturgical arguments for at least considering the provision of some liturgical form for the blessing of a marriage of those whose faith is not sufficient for the celebration of a sacrament.

Reintegrating liturgy and service is in one sense easier, in that it does not have to wait upon the deliberations of canonists and theologians, or the policy decisions of bishops, or the statistical collapse of the priesthood in 1990. It requires no more than the conviction of priests or other individuals and their ability to communicate it to the rest of the worshipping community and to carry them with them. That may sound anything but easy, but it can be done, as has been shown in a number of parishes up and down the country but perhaps nowhere more impressively than at Our Lady of the Wayside at Shirley in the West Midlands. The parish priest, Patrick O'Mahony, has described in a recent book how a very ordinary suburban parish has mobilized itself to raise hundreds of thousands of pounds for the Third World; to monitor human rights and adopt prisoners of conscience in all corners of the world; to collect, sort and dispatch tons of medical supplies to underdeveloped countries; to welcome immigrants, improve race relations, help the aged, house the homeless and care for the handicapped in their own locality. And this not in one-off campaigns, but year in, year out. 'There was a real need in Shirley,' he says, 'to alter the stance and commitment of the majority of people.

So often they are isolated, introspective and pietistic; seldom does their Christianity inform their secular lives in any integral way. Much work is needed and, in our case, three or four years were spent in preparatory work before we were able to effect anything worthwhile.'[15] In any number of parishes one can find SVP or Justice and Peace groups involved in action of this sort; what is needed is to raise the awareness of the whole community to see that these concerns cannot be left to small groups acting in its name, but are the responsibility of the parish as a whole. 'The Church must be the place where justice is happening', and this conviction comes directly from the experience of the liturgy, and particularly the Mass 'where caring and sharing are at their highest point.... I myself believe the most dynamic vision and political statement of our time is the Eucharist which teaches that, in spite of the standards of a consumer society which is dominated by possessions, everything we have is on loan for a short time... and that as God our Father shares his daily bread with us, so we should share with one another, whoever we are and wherever we live.'[16]

Already it should be quite evident that the developments I have envisaged demand a rethinking of the deployment we make of personnel and resources, and of priorities at every level of the Church, especially among priests: 'The People of God is formed into one in the first place by the Word of the living God... Priests, as co-workers with their bishops, have as their primary duty the proclamation of the gospel of God.'[17] The rolling programme of formation that I have advocated is something for which priests will have neither the confidence nor the aptitude. It need not, indeed could not, depend on them for its entire conception and execution, but it must have their wholehearted encouragement and support, and assume the principal place in their priorities. It will certainly take them away from other things, worthwhile things. The formation and maintenance of a community is certainly a prime objective of priestly work, but not a ghetto community, nor simply a community of mutual support. It must be a community of faith, witness and service, and neither home-visiting, fund-raising, social organization nor even Sunday Mass and its homilies will be sufficient to achieve this. Other ministries to the community, whether officially recognized and commissioned or not, will be indispensable to this object: teachers, parents, group-leaders, and above all catechists who must be professionally trained, paid and full-time. Their work will never be finished. Most important of all is the rediscovery of the diaconal ministry—not at all that of cultic deacons, but that of the whole community which exists, like Christ himself, to lose itself in care, concern and service. People visiting or transporting the sick, manning a picket, packing parcels for India, writing letters to prisoners, must realise that they are not on their own, freelancing do-gooders, but are the agents of the Church, exercising in a real way the ministry of the Servant Christ, building up his Body, mediating his presence to the world, extending in time and space the worship of God.

A congregation so organized and operating will almost certainly require a somewhat different sort of premises from those in which it currently assembles. It will realise that it is itself the Body of Christ and the living temple of the living God. When it possesses buildings, these should be not just a shelter for worship but a meeting place for the assembly in all its activities, an appropriate base for formation, for community action, for mission and service. We have far too many churches which are fit for nothing whatsoever but formal worship, and no longer even very fit for that. They do not even facilitate the celebrating of liturgy together, much less the mixing together which is the basis of any community, and not at all the sharing together of God's Word and growth together in faith, or the service of neighbourhood and world, all of which should distinguish any Christian community which is faithful to its Master. A most heartening trend in recent years has been the unwillingness of many communities to spend vast sums of money on buildings which serve liturgy in isolation and perpetuate its dissociation from evangelization and service. An appropriate house for God's people will include space not only for formal worship but for the formation which precedes and underpins it (in meeting rooms, libraries, bookshops, etc) and for the action and service which flows from it (in day-centres, playgroups, youth centres, over-60s clubs, counselling rooms, etc). Several good examples now exist.

In my opinion, it is only when these priorities are accepted and developments of this sort are being worked upon that many of the conventional, internal concerns of 'liturgy' come into perspective and their discussion becomes tolerable. To fill the letter columns of the press week after week with ill-tempered arguments over the merits of this or that translation, while millions in the world, through lack of access to education, are illiterate in any language, is an obscenity. To haggle and vilify each other over communion in the hand or communion in the mouth, when millions of our starving brothers have nothing in their hands or their mouths, is a near blasphemy—sacrifices without mercy, saying 'Lord, Lord', honouring him with our lips while our hearts are far from him. God is not given glory by sacred words or mysterious rituals, no matter how ancient, poetic or beautifully performed, but only by people who believe more fully, who love him and their neighbour more deeply, who help each other to grow into what God has called them to be.

I do not wish to imply that the texts and rites of the liturgy are unimportant, but I do strongly insist that the criteria for assessing and comparing them should be primarily pastoral rather than aesthetic. Which means, first of all, that we should be concerned more about the content of the prayers than their language or style. And here I think there is a very great need for enrichment and improvement, so that, for instance, the values and perspectives of Vatican II's *Gaudium et Spes* ('the joys and the hopes, the griefs and the anguish of the men of our time, especially the poor and afflicted') may find expression not just in the odd votive Mass but in the regular worship of the Sunday assembly. It means, secondly, an attention to form, not in the sense of the rules of classical prosody, but in recovering the laws and skills of oral not written communication. Our present liturgy—and even more so its English critics, perhaps mesmerised by Cranmer—seem often to be prisoners of the written word, whereas genuine liturgy derives from another tradition: of story-telling, creative proclamation, and direct spoken communication. All of which points to the conclusion that our texts will never be entirely satisfactory until they are original compositions in English rather than translations,[18] as it is difficult to conceive how one can really compose a living liturgy in a dead language. But then one has to face the question: what sort of English? We exist, not only in the English-speaking world, but within England, and indeed within any parish in England, in a situation of cultural heterogeneity, which we may lament but may not escape. Should the liturgy express the faith and understanding, the response and commitment of the congregation in the language of ecclesiastical tradition, or of a literary élite, or of the mass media, or of the pop culture? It is no use simply wringing our hands over the corruption of language or the slippage of academic standards. Ministers of the liturgy are not the agents of a 'clerisy', custodians of an intellectual or cultural heritage, curators of a museum, and they should respectfully ignore letters to *The Times* or to the pope by outraged *literati* and representatives of the cultural establishment. To simplify the issues rather crudely: we should ask of a text not 'will this entice Sir Michael Tippett to compose a setting for us?' but 'will it inspire Fred Jones to put in an hour with meals on wheels or the CAFOD collection?'.

One wishes that as much vigilance and concern had been shown for the symbols and actions of the liturgy as for the words. The integrity of our celebrations has been far more fundamentally damaged by the attenuation or misuse of symbols than by any inaccuracy or infelicity of translation. At the time of writing, a welcome lifeboat has been launched, with a concerted campaign from the Liturgical Commission to restore the integrity of the signs in the Eucharist, bread and wine, eating and drinking, breaking and sharing. The crisis of credibility with which we began is intimately bound up with the crisis of symbolism. Unlike words, symbols speak to our whole personality, not just to our ears and intelligences; they create resonances and associations inaccessible to words, they appeal to intuition and experience as much as to understanding. And their power is incomparably greater than any words. It is sad, then, to see so many celebrants tackling the alienation within the liturgy by resorting to more and more words with less and less effect, while allowing the symbols to shrink to the point of total insignificance if not downright countersignificance. A renewed reverence for symbols, letting them speak with their full power, would do much to purify our words, challenge our experience, and bring together again expression and reality. Words, action, experience, in proper harmony mean an integrated liturgy.

Evangelization, catechesis, formal liturgy, service of neighbour, daily living, all constitute the worship of God as understood and commended by St Paul. Service of God in our neighbour and service of God in the liturgy, worship of God in our everyday lives and worship of God in church, are not alternatives that we are free to choose between according to taste, but two complementary, mutually evocative forms of one Christian worship; and each is incomplete and inauthentic without the other. Our liturgy will only be true and authentic if it expresses in celebration a genuine response in faith, love and service—a response which we make and live in the whole of our lives. If we are a truly Christian community, then the whole of our life, our work, our relationships, our politics, will be revealing Christ to us, putting us in contact with him, and evoking from us a response to him. Our liturgy is prepared, and validated, by the quality of our relationships, by the depth of our concern for the poor and the oppressed, by the spirit of love, joy, acceptance and service which shines out of our community and extends to all mankind. It is through these in the first place that we, and others through us, will experience God and his love and respond to him in faith. The more powerful this experience and response, the more it will demand full expression and strengthening in the celebration of the liturgy. Then, indeed, God will have mercy and sacrifice; we will be honouring him not only with our lips but with our lives as well:

Non clamor sed amor cantat in aure Dei.

Notes

1   'Mobilising for Renewal', *Music and Liturgy*, Winter 1975.

2   J. Gelineau, *The Liturgy Today and Tomorrow*, E.T. London, 1978, p. 121

3   Witness and evangelization: Rom 1:9; 15:16; charity and service of neighbour: 2 Cor 9:11-13; Phil 4:18; everything in life without exception: Col 3:17; 1 Tim 4:4; Rom 12:1 and *passim.*

4   For the fullest treatment, see A. Hamman, *Vie liturgique, Vie sociale*, Paris, 1968.

5   A beginning has been made with the report of the joint working-party of the Bishops' Conference and the National Conference of Priests of England and Wales, *A Time for Building*, 1976.

6   Vatican II, Constitution on the Sacred Liturgy, 9.

7   *Op. cit.*, p. 42

8   'Accompagnement ecclésiologique pour les assemblées dominicales sans célébration eucharistique', *La Maison-Dieu* 130, 1977, p. 121.

9   Cf. Hamman, *op. cit.*; E. Schillebeeckx, 'Secular Worship and Church Liturgy', *God the Future of Man*, London, 1969; G. Wainwright, 'The Risks and Possibilities of Liturgical Reform', *Studia Liturgica* 8/2, 1971-2; H. Gollwitzer, *The Rich Christians and Poor Lazarus*, Edinburgh, 1970; T. Cullinan, *Eucharist and Politics*, London, 1973; J.G. Davies, *Worship and Mission*, London, 1966.

10 A fine example is the official programme of the diocese of Brooklyn (USA), *Initiation into a Eucharistic Community*, Brooklyn, 1973, which I describe in my article 'Mobilising for Renewal' (cf. note above).

11 Cf. the entire issue of *La Maison-Dieu* 130, 1977.

12 Sacred Congregation for Divine Worship, *Directory on Masses with Children*, 1973.

13 *Op. cit.*, chapter 4.

14 Cf. my chapter in H. Winstone (ed.), *Pastoral Liturgy*, London, 1975.

15 P.J. O'Mahony, *The Fantasy of Human Rights*, Great Wakering, 1978, p. 58

16 *Op. cit.*, pp. 60, 151

17 Vatican II, Decree on the Priestly Life, 4.

18 They should also be adaptable, through creative interpretation and reworking, to the needs of oral communication: cf. J. Gelineau, *op. cit.*, chapters 8, 11, and J.D. Crichton, *The Once and the Future Liturgy*, Dublin, 1977, chapter 4.

Appendix

Dom Bernard McElligott OSB, 1890-1971

J.D. Crichton

(The most complete memoir of Bernard McElligott will be found in the Ampleforth Journal, *Summer and Autumn, vol. LXXVII, parts ii and iii, pp. 102-9; pp. 85-97. The author is Dom Alberic Stacpoole whose principal sources are the Ampleforth records and conversations with Dom Bernard in his last years. Where quotations appear in the following appreciation, they are taken, with permission, from the above articles. The minute-books and the magazine of the Society of St Gregory have supplied further information.)*

Bernard McElligott is not an easy man to write about. For much of his life he appeared as a man of action who was quite widely known, yet he always gave the impression of being a private man. To most he seemed withdrawn, a man who thought his own thoughts, who, always courteous, did not make contacts easily. He had little small-talk, though his charming smile won many. Yet he was capable of intimacy and sought it, and those who were able to establish a friendship with him—and there seemed to have been many—found him delightful company and rapidly came to love him. He was certainly a quiet man—obtrusive noises were physically painful to him—and quite typical of him is the story told of him as he appeared in all the swirl of a summer school: 'Insistent as he was when rehearsing, he afterwards returned to being the smiling, self-effacing cleric at the table of the humbler members—"Who is that quiet priest over there? Him? He is our President".' Quiet he may have been, yet he was filled with a consuming energy that from time to time broke down a constitution which, in the second half of his life, was never robust. Combined with this drive and a great tenacity was an extraordinarily sensitive nature, a mixture that brought him a good deal of suffering and probably drove him in on himself. Modest and withdrawn, somewhat hesistant in his approach to others, in a way self-centred, he was unaware of the esteem and affection in which he was held, especially in his later years by his own community.

Born in Glasgow in 1890, he was christened John and was known (improbably as it seems to us) to his contemporaries as 'Jack'. At what now seems to be the early age of ten he went to Ampleforth.

In the light of his later development, his school days offer some surprises. He took a full part in every kind of school activity, games—he was captain of Set II in both soccer and cricket—the debating society and the dramatic society, 'earning praise for his parts as Mrs Bouncer in the farce *Box and Cox* and as Socrates in *The Clouds*'. Nor did his academic record suffer from this many-sided activity. He passed the public examinations with distinction at a quite early age, showing proficiency especially in Latin, Greek and French. But he had already been absorbing Shakespeare and won a prize for an essay on 'The English Historical Plays'. Even in later life he was able to quote freely from Shakespeare and seemed to know whole tracts of him by heart. It was perhaps his first response to beauty.

With a successful school career behind him, he chose to enter the community and made his novitiate at Belmont, then common to the English Benedictine Congregation. He was not alone in finding the Belmont novitiate difficult. It was a grim time for all: the house 'was cold without proper heating, spartan without good food' and the young monks had to do all the cleaning. Unfortunately Bernard (he received this name when he was 'clothed') had not given much thought to his vocation and 'had no clear idea about the life,... did not know what he wanted or why he became a monk'. But he held on—an example of his tenacity—and was simply professed and received minor orders at Belmont from John Cuthbert Hedley, Bishop of Newport and Menevia and a revered member of the Ampleforth community.

In 1910 he passed to Oxford to read Honour Moderations and 'Greats'. Here he came to a more congenial life, although little seems to have been recorded of his days there. But in Fr Bede Jarrett OP, who understood the young and who built up a whole philosophy of Christian friendship, and who gave the Michaelmas and Hilary term conferences, he must have found a kindred spirit. In 1914, just before the war began, he graduated and returned to Ampleforth to teach classics and in fact to continue his cultivation of English literature.

Quite soon, in 1915, he was asked to take over the music of the house. So the man who had a certain aptitude for the cello but was without any professional training in music and, as he himself was well aware, without a singing voice, was presented with a challenge which he rose to. As a chronicler of the time records: in a few months he 'acquired the conductor's manner, which insists so vigorously and protests so much that it commands the obedience of wayward youth'.

These first years were happy ones. He had something to do that he could do and wanted to do. Not that he was not successful in his teaching, but all through his life he had an almost overwhelming love of music and he loved getting people to sing. That he greatly improved the quality and style of the music of the house is beyond doubt, though there can be few now who felt the first impact of his enthusiasm. But Dom Bernard was a perfectionist and, like all perfectionists, he was unwittingly voracious of other people's time and energies. He was also sensitive, he responded very strongly to the beauty of literature and to the beauty of music but, perhaps especially at this time of his life, he did not understand why all his fellow-monks did not respond similarly. Others in the community, equally gifted, did not have his sensibility or at least he thought they had not. Tensions, it seems, grew; and, since he had now taught for thirteen years, it was no doubt thought that a change might do him good. By 1927 he found himself 'on the parish' at St Mary's Priory, Canton, Cardiff. If ever any man was *not* cut out for parish life, it was Bernard McElligott, and he was not happy either then or later when in 1941 he returned there. Of visiting the people he was heard to murmur 'I don't know what to talk about'. Bach and *The Tempest* would hardly have provided suitable opening gambits.

Nevertheless it was just at this time that he conceived the notion of a society for mutual assistance in the singing of church music and for the improving of its quality generally. What prompted him to do this does not seem to have been recorded. Evidently he had been pondering the *Motu proprio* of Pius X, and *Divini Cultus* came in time to confirm his purpose when he inaugurated the Society of St Gregory. This was to prove his dominant interest for the rest of his life; it was to bring him into the limelight; it would bring him in touch with all kinds of people, some important like Cardinal Hinsley; and through his work for the Society he became involved in broadcasting. With the exception of a short time during the second war, his life henceforth was a very busy one until 1951, when he surrendered the executive leadership of the Society.

The work of the Society is described elsewhere in this book; here we are concerned with his impact on it. It would be too harsh to say that Dom Bernard dominated it, but he was certainly its mainspring; and quiet though he was, his presence was palpable. In some ways he could be described as a gentle dictator, though his strength lay not in organization—much less in ordering people about—but in his convictions and in his inflexible determination to forward the aims of the Society, namely to promote the active participation of the people and to raise the standard of church music in this country. Church authority had said that active participation should be fostered and the chief means (then) was to be the singing of plainsong. This is what he set out to put into effect, and in the long view it must be said that he had a considerable success. His success might have been greater if he had not insisted so inflexibly on the virtues of plainsong and had not shown an indifference to other music (except polyphony) which might the more easily have achieved the end he had in view. Likewise his perfectionism limited the range of his work. Perhaps in his earlier days he transmitted an enthusiasm that was catching, but in later years his general rehearsals were painstaking to the point of being laborious. He took too much time to cover too little ground, and relied overmuch on a limited repertoire of anecdotes.

In the period before lectures on liturgy were begun, he addressed the summer school at the beginning and the end; and here again in the early years he aroused enthusiasm. But for a man who was soaked in English literature and who usually wrote clearly and with force, it was curious to find that he was not a ready speaker. He did not give the impression that he had marshalled his thoughts (though he had) and he took a long time to say little. When, however, he lectured from a script, he was almost always worth listening to. Perhaps for this reason he took readily to broadcasting, a medium that suited him and his musical interests, though he insisted on learning the right techniques in which he became something of an expert. He did a little journalism and his articles were clearly and simply written. Whatever he said or wrote was deeply pondered for it was the fruit of thought. He was a thoughtful man even if his range was not very wide.

When in 1942 a change of policy in the work of the Society arose, the initiative almost certainly came from Dom Bernard. As will be recalled, lectures on the liturgy were to be introduced into the summer school programme and the reason (or *a* reason) for this is to be found in the Minute-Book: 'The question of a Summer School was then raised (there had been none in 1940 and 1941)... It was suggested that it might take the form of a liturgical week, and that the first of the Society's Four Aims should be specially stressed. This could be more usefully done now, as the musical activities in many Churches are, of necessity, much restricted owing to war conditions...'. A reflection of this situation is to be found in the introduction of the Dialogue Mass that was used at this Summer School or at the 1943 School. Here again, Dom Bernard became something of an expert; and a Dialogue Mass that he had practised was a very different thing from the almost inaudible mutterings that did duty for it in other places later on.

The lecture programme was almost certainly shaped by Dom Bernard though no doubt with the help of the committee. When *Mediator Dei* appeared in 1947 it gave him a new impetus; and, just as he had tirelessly expounded the somewhat meagre liturgical content of the two previous papal documents, so now he expounded the new. It became the basis of his lectures to many and various audiences for a long time to come. In connection with this, and because he realised the importance of *Mediator Dei*, he took another initiative and founded the Priests' Association of the Society of St Gregory. It was to be a means by which priests, gathered together from time to time, could study the doctrine of the encyclical in greater depth and to introduce it to those who were ignorant of it. But in the interests of history it should be said that at the first meeting at Bishton Hall in Staffordshire, it looked very much as if there were to be no further meetings. It was thanks to pressure from certain priests who were there that it was agreed that further meetings should be held. Unhappily the number attending was always small. The Society of St Gregory was indelibly printed in the minds of most of the clergy as an association for the singing of plainsong—just that!—and it proved difficult to attract those who most needed it to study the liturgy.

In instituting a lecture programme for the summer school, Dom Bernard had brought into existence a child that would outgrow his expectations; and when, in the later 1940s and early fifties, the pressure for a more pastoral emphasis became apparent, he did not seem to be so happy. *Nothing* was to be allowed to interfere with or diminish the plainsong programme; and it was sometimes difficult to harmonize the demands of those who wanted lectures/discussions and those who wanted to maintain the by-now traditional quota of plainsong. But it was typical of the man that he made no protests (though he did press his point strongly in committee) and it was certainly not the tensions in the Society that led him to resign the Vice-Presidency in 1951. His health, always precarious, was giving trouble, and operations did nothing to restore his old energies. He became an Honorary Member of the committee and usually attended its meetings. Almost always he appeared at the summer schools and, when necessary, took rehearsals in both plainsong and polyphony. He had lost nothing of his old skill but the effort visibly exhausted him.

Although his biographer is of the opinion that Dom Bernard was 'an ardent supporter of the new changes, whatever they did to outdate his work' (p. 95), it is not an easy matter to assess his reactions to the Constitution on the Liturgy and all that came in its wake. He could of course see that the Constitution gave an enormous impetus to that active participation for which he had preached and striven for more than thirty years. Indeed, by allowing the use of the people's language in the celebration of the liturgy it made that participation possible for millions of people throughout the world. But three things, it seems, gave him cause for concern. The position of plainsong was obviously threatened and that was someting he dearly loved. The poor quality of the music at first provided to accompany the new rite can hardly have pleased him, and as representative of the Society with the Church Music Association he actively concerned himself with the matter. Thirdly, with his love of beauty, especially in words, the somewhat drab translations that were offered must have been painful to him. But it was precisely the matter of the nature of active participation that gave him most concern. This, at the time (the middle 1960s), was understandable, for those who had but recently been all in favour of silence now began to insist on vocal participation, sometimes in ways that suggested regimentation. Dom Bernard, then, tackled this question anew in a long paper that he read to the 1969 summer school. He made much of the distinction, derived from the earlier papal document, between a *participatio activa* and a *participatio actuosa*, the latter signifying for him a participation that was indeed active but which at the same time should be interior. It was a remarkably vigorous performance for a man in his late seventies, and spoke with unusual passion; but it is curious that he did not make more of the teaching of the Constitution that participation must be 'full, *conscious* and *devout*' (nos. 14, 48)—that is, interior.

However that may be, the theme, which he often repeated elsewhere around this time, witnesses to a quality of his life that might otherwise pass unnoticed. Dom Bernard spent many years of his life promoting the people's share in liturgical celebration by the singing of plainsong and by Dialogue Masses. The superficial might have thought—and some did think—that he was concerned with externals. But his writings, his lectures, all his teaching are evidence of his conviction that these methods were no more than means to an end, namely the prayerful offering of the Mass, though he saw plainsong itself as a mode of prayer. As he said in his first address to the first summer school, 'Plainsong is prayer'. It was so for him, and it can be seen as an indication of his own life of prayer which could be glimpsed when he celebrated Mass. Active participation, as he understood it, was an expression of *his* interior life, and he wished to share with others the same experience. Nor was this all. Although he was a nervy person, there always seemed to be a still centre in him that, one may speculate, came from his contemplation of God in and through the beauty that he saw as a reflection of the God who had created it.

Dom Bernard had lived in many places in the course of his life but by 1963, now old, tired and unwell, 'to the delight of his brethren, who had much to gain from his wisdom, he decided to return to the Abbey... and live out his last days with us'. These last years were indeed something of an Indian summer for him. He found support and stimulus in the community to whom he gave a number of talks. But he also seems to have been rejuvenated, for he travelled to Westminster to address the diocesan clergy there as well as nearer home to speak to those of the Middlesbrough diocese. His life's work received a certain recognition with his appointment to the National Commission for Catholic Church Music and this brought him into contact with the National Liturgical Commission. Finally, his visits to Stanbrook Abbey in 1968 to help in choir training were a source of joy both to him and to the nuns.

Thus full of years and works he came towards his end. 'He was conscious that he was dying; and gentle, shy, essentially private as he was, he made his own peace with characteristic serenity. His last days were lived in the care of someone long close to his heart. He died just before Christmas 1971, murmuring *Gloria Patri, et Filio, et Spiritui... .*' A Requiem Mass for him was celebrated on 3 March, St Aelred's Day, in Westminster Cathedral, and at the end of it was sung the *Christus vincit* from the thirteenth century Worcester Antiphoner, a chant that had ended every summer school for years.

We cannot do better than close this appreciation with words uttered at the funeral Mass by the Abbot (now Cardinal Hume) on 29 December 1971: 'We admired your gift of friendship and received much from it. How well you could speak of love; there was nothing trite or possessive or sentimental in what you said and it reflected the practice which you had learnt over the years. You had seen and then taught others that human love is a way to arrive at an understanding of the love of God. We learnt from you that sensitivity to beauty in all its forms is a way to God because you showed us that the beauty of God is to be found revealed in the beauty of His creation. No wonder that you found in Teilhard de Chardin a mind which was very like your own. We shared your keenness to fathom, as far as it lies in the human mind to do so, the mystery of the Mass. We shall remember your insistence that it should be surrounded with dignity and beauty. Others will speak with more authority of your great contribution in the field of music, but we acknowledge in our Community the work that you did and the influence you had on us.' *Ampleforth Journal*, Spring 1972 (Vol. LXXVII, i), p. 114. Perhaps no better epitaph could be suggested than that placed by Dom Alberic Stacpoole at the end of his memoir:

> Remember me for this, my God; do not blot out the pious deed I have done for the Temple of God and for its liturgy.

(*Nehemiah 13:14*)

Index of Names